When God Works
INCOGNITO
Autobiographical Vignettes

*(Thoughts and Memories of
My Life and Lifetime)*

Keep Walking by Faith
Fred Beck
Proverbs 3:5+6

FRED BECK

ISBN 978-1-64191-475-8 (paperback)
ISBN 978-1-64191-476-5 (digital)

Christian Faith Publishing, Inc.
832 Park Avenue
Meadville, PA 16335
www.christianfaithpublishing.com

Printed in the United States of America

To the loves of my life: my wife, Linda, and our adult children: Pamela, Stephen, Micah, and Matthew, and their families, including all our grandchildren and great-grandchildren.

Contents

Corrie ten Boom said, "Memories are the key not to the past, but to the future." Jim Denison concurs by saying, "All our Lord has done, He can still do." Hebrews 13:8 says, "Jesus Christ is the same yesterday and today and (yes) forever."

Thus, I humbly offer these autobiographical vignettes of my life and lifetime ...

Preface

The word *grace* (unmerited favor) is the most beautiful and meaningful concept on earth. God's grace has many facets: mercy, love, forgiveness, renewal, worth, hope, security, etc.

God is so good. I have personally experienced His goodness. I have experienced it directly from God Himself as well as indirectly through many people. God has graced others who have in turn graced me. They graced me by their love and forgiveness, even though my sin and my rough edges caused them personal pain and loss. For some, that pain and suffering was great. Most important among those are my parents, siblings, wife, and children. But countless friends and acquaintances have also graced me.

I am a sinner, who has been saved by God's grace alone, with no merit on my part. Grace is an undeserved gift. God's grace has forgiven me and has changed me. It also enables me to forgive others, even as I am forgiven by God. The Bible says that all who are "in Christ" are "a new creation." That does not make me a perfect or superior person, but neither am I the person that I once was. That is only one of the reasons that I love God so much. The Bible states, "He who has been forgiven much, loves much."

I must take responsibility for my sin and shortcomings. However, God has taken the initiative and responsibility for forgiving and for the process of recreating me in the image of Jesus and thereby prepare me to live forever with Him, in eternity. Grace is the totality of what God has done, is presently doing, and will do, in order to complete His purpose for sinful people like me, who put their trust in Him.

That is why *grace* is the most beautiful word I know, as well as the most wonderful and renewing thing I have experienced.

Birth and Early Years

The *Great Depression* began after the stock market crash of October 1929. It ushered in more than a decade of economic collapse. Hundreds of thousands of people became destitute and were fed in food kitchens established to feed the hungry. Most Americans became poor. Perhaps the farmers were the lucky ones; at least they had food to eat. However, many of them also lost everything during the Dust Bowl years.

The grip of economic depression and desperation would not end until after much of our navy was devastated in December 7, 1941. The surprise Japanese air attack on Pearl Harbor, Hawaii, plunged us into a war that we did not want. It became a war fought in different theaters, against enemies from different regions (Germany and its allies in Europe and north Africa, and Japan in the Asia-Pacific region). However, pursuit of victory in "the war" (WWII) created an industrial boom that brought an end to "the Great Depression."

Late in that depression era, I was born in Gainesville, Florida, on the Labor Day evening, Monday, September 5, 1938. I am the eldest of five children (Fred, Clair III, Wayne, Sharon, and Brenda). I was named after my great-grandfather, George Jacob Bishop, Sr. My Mom told me that my middle name, Frederick, was the name of the doctor who delivered me. As was the custom in Mom's family, I was called by my middle name: Freddy when I was young, Frederick or George Frederick when they were upset with me, and Fred when I got older.

My parents were Clair Matthew Beck Jr. and Gladys Elese "Elese" Bishop Beck. Dad was born in Riverside, California, on February 6, 1916; Mom in Hampton County, South Carolina, on February 26, 1920. They were married in Gainesville, Florida, on February 16, 1938. I don't know, but I assume my parents met at First Baptist Church.

Hugh Gladys Earl?
Elese - Dorothy Miriam
7   5   3

My paternal grandparents were Clair Matthew Beck Sr. and Mary Edna "Edna" Clark Beck. Granddad Beck was born January 24, 1894, in Monticello, White County, Indiana. Grandmother Beck was

born March 5, 1889, in Trenton, New Jersey. They were married June 27, 1914, in Riverside, California, and had six children: Clair Jr. (my dad), Eleanor, Donald, Betty, Doris and Harry. All the children were born in California. At the time of my birth, they lived either in Gainesville or Jay, Florida.

My maternal grandparents were Henry Hugh "Hugh" Bishop, and Lila Gladys "Gladys" (Connelly) Bishop. Dada (Granddad Bishop) was born December 12, 1899, in Hampton County, South Carolina. Mama (Grandmother Bishop), born October 12, 1903, was also from Hampton County, South Carolina. They were married in Hampton on April 6, 1919. They had five children. Elese (my mom), Dorothy, Miriam, Russell, and Earl. Both boys died in childhood. After my mom's birth, they moved to Gainesville, Florida, after Mama's father gave them land, where they resided most of the rest of their lives.

The April 1940 US Census, five months prior to my second birthday reveals that we lived with my mom's parents and that Dad was an insurance salesman. When I was two, Mom, Dad and I lived in a rented house, near downtown Gainesville. Dad was a salesman in a nearby jewelry store.

I was nearly killed when I fell from the car driven by my mom's youngest sister, Miriam. We were on Glenn Springs Road, in a "Nash" and the rear doors opened from front to back (suicide doors). Apparently, I opened the door slightly, and the wind flung the door completely open and me with it. The road was paved with slag, a very rough stone. I still bear two small scars from that accident: one on my right thumb and another on my left shoulder.

I suffered nightmares for many years, even into adulthood. I assume they were based on that accident. In my dreams, my whole body swelled up and floated away. I don't remember any actual thoughts of pain in the dreams. However, the frequency and intensity of those dreams lessened over the years. The last one I experienced was in the 1990s (when I was over fifty years old).

As an adult, I learned, from my great-aunt Jessie (Auntie) and some others, that even though we were poor, *I was somewhat pampered (first child, first grandchild, first nephew). Actually, I was spoiled rotten and very selfish.* As I think about that, it was obviously true, for I can remember many very selfish moments during my childhood and what I did to get what I wanted. One glaring example: when I was eight, on several occasions, I stole pocket change from my dad's trousers to buy candy. I was a true son of "the first Adam," but rejoice, the "second Adam" paid for my sin, gave me a new spirit, and I was adopted by our Heavenly Father.

Later my family moved in with my mom's parents again. Dad was a good carpenter and helped Granddad Bishop (Dada) add on to their house. *Mom, Dad, and I lived in the barn, and the pump house became our kitchen.* I do not remember my brother Clair's birth on March 21, 1941. I do remember being frightened when a snake got into our barn bedroom. Dad quickly dispatched the reptile by cutting off its head with a hatchet.

My fondest memories in Gainesville were of my family, including grandparents (Bishop) and aunts. I thought that my Dada "hung the moon." Dada had a bird dog with a rusty red coat. His name was Red. Red and I were buddies.

I was also fond of playing with Bobby Guy, a second cousin four years my senior. Bobby lived about a half mile up the unpaved sandy road with his mom (our Aunt Jessie, whom everyone called Auntie). Actually, they lived with his grandparents (my great-grandparents), Ben and Elizabeth (DeLoach) Connelly.

When at Bobby's house, all play stopped in the afternoon to listen to *Superman, The Lone Ranger*, etc., on the radio.

 Bobby's hobby was building model airplanes. He purchased kits and used balsa wood to construct the frame then used tissue paper as the plane's skin. I thought that was really neat. *Bobby was my idol.* While talking with Bobby in 2002, I thanked him for putting up with his younger cousin. Bobby admitted that it was good to have me around because there were very few other kids living close by.

One not-too-pleasant memory was the time Bobby was playing at "my house." He "decided to go home." I got angry because he left, so I climbed a fence and cut across the pasture and hid behind a bush. When the road circled around the field and Bobby passed by, I threw a rock and hit him. He chased me back home. Because he had to climb a barbed wire fence, I had a head start and won the race home. However, Mama made that victory short-lived when she broke off several switches from the hedge and "wore them out" on my legs.

A common summer social event everyone enjoyed was having neighbors over to talk, usually outdoors, in the early evening. Sometimes we boiled peanuts in an old backyard black cast-iron washing pot. We were dirt poor; nevertheless, they were happy days. Dada Bishop grew peanuts and watermelon on his land. I don't remember other crops. He had at least one milk cow, and Mama raised chickens.

At some point in time, Dada began working for a "moss" company. He drove a company truck on country routes buying dried Spanish moss. That was before foam rubber was invented. The moss was used as stuffing in furniture and in automobile seats.

The moss was gathered from trees by both poor whites and poor African Americans. Dada gave them the wire to bale it for easier handling. Dada went on a different route each weekday of the month, repeating those routes each month. One summer when I was nearly ten years old, I accompanied Dada on the moss route a few times. That was a special treat for me.

Racial prejudice was much worse then than today. African Americans were politely referred to as Negroes, or colored people. In those terrible days of racial segregation, there were separate and usually inferior schools, restrooms, drinking fountains, etc., for blacks. It was against the law for them to use "white facilities." They could not eat in white cafes, and when they rode public buses, they had to sit in the back of the bus; even then they had to give up their rear seat if a white didn't have a seat.

Blacks were also relegated to low-paying jobs in the labor and service sectors—i.e. domestic household workers, janitorial jobs in industry, etc. In the agriculture sector, some were subsistence share croppers while others picked cotton or other menial harvesting tasks to earn money.

Not all whites were prejudiced toward African Americans. Many other whites were not unkind to them, but their prejudice showed through statements like, "Colored folk are good people. I don't have anything against them, *as long as they stay in their place.*"

My Granddad Bishop and his siblings had been cared for by a young black lady for a couple of years after their mother died.

I do not remember knowing any black children during my ten years in Florida. I remember seeing black convicts cutting the grass and weeds, with hand tools, along the highway in Jay, Florida. I also remember picking cotton alongside black people. However, blacks were not allowed to live in Jay. There was a common, but horrible, saying, "Black man, don't let the sun set on your back in Jay, Florida."

Even after we moved to Galveston, Texas, in 1948, our schools were still segregated. I saw many African Americans but did not know any personally. That changed when my mom started working out of the home. Mom and Dad hired Classie Mae (Mrs. J. B. Whitaker), a black lady, to watch us kids, in their absence. Classie Mae also did light house cleaning, washing, and ironing. She went home after I returned home from school and could watch my younger siblings.

Classie Mae lived a couple of miles from us but walked to and from our house; her salary was small, and she could not afford to waste any on transportation. She was a chain smoker and very overweight. She had been married many years but had not been able to have children. Well, not until several years later, when they were surprised with a son. All of us loved Classie Mae. However, as my younger siblings got older and didn't need as much care, Mom and Dad had to let her go. They too needed all the money they made to make ends meet at home.

Several years later, after I graduated from high school and was employed as an electric meter reader, I sometimes saw Classie Mae when I read her meter. She always insisted that I come in and let her prepare something for me to eat. Her son was a handful. He was spoiled rotten, even as I had been.

What a terrible irony that we Americans, who prize freedom, ever bought into slavery. America was "the land of the free" for everyone except for the African slaves, who were regarded, by some, as less than human.

Even after their emancipation from slavery, they were usually treated like second- or third-class citizens.

*The Civil War (called the War of Rebellion by many in the North and the War of Aggression by most in the South) was drawing to a close when Abraham Lincoln ran for a second term, as president. This time, Lincoln chose Andrew Johnson, of Tennessee, to be his running mate; thus Johnson became vice president after their victory. Although Johnson was a Southerner, he lost all Southern support when he supported Lincoln, who was hated by the South for freeing the slaves and for other political and constitutional grievances.

When I was young, the South was referred to as "the solid South," meaning it was solidly Democrat. It was the Republicans who freed the slaves and invaded the South. The Democrats were proslavery, and even after the conclusion of the Civil War, they maintained laws of segregation and passed laws to keep blacks subservient to whites.

As eventual victory by the "Union" became evident Lincoln did not want to "rub the South's face in the mud," after the coming defeat of the Confederacy. However, the assassination of President Lincoln, only a month into his second term, changed all of that.

Thus, a short time after becoming vice president, Johnson became president. Perhaps Johnson intended to follow Lincoln's plan for leniency and reconstruction for the South. *However, he met heavy opposition, and in the end, he allowed the punishment of the South to take place. In my estimation, from a "Southern perspective," that set race relations and national reunion back a hundred years.*

This is not to justify the South, but the post–Civil War punitive actions of the federal government flamed continued hatred in the South. When I was young, people had a tongue-in-cheek saying, "Save your Confederate money, the South will rise again." It was a joke; nonetheless, it tugged the heartstrings of Southerners. Like it or not, I have been influenced by my Southern heritage. I also believe the continued use of the Confederate flag, the singing of "Dixie," etc., were also prolonged by the hatred of the "Northern Carpetbaggers." As a young boy, I thought "Damn Yankee" was one word.

Larry Mills, a retired Baptist pastor friend of mine, shared a new insight about President Andrew Johnson, which seems to reveal that Johnson was not as bad as I thought.

The scene is the Senate Chamber of the United States Congress. The issue at stake is the impeachment of President Andrew Johnson, who became president upon the assassination of Abraham Lincoln. The Radical Republicans, who control Congress, hate Johnson because they thought he was being too easy on the South and because he continued to veto bills they tried to push through. So the House of Representatives impeached him on what were essentially trumped-up charges of a strictly political nature. Now the vote was in the senate. They needed a two-thirds vote to impeach Johnson. Everyone's vote was set, and the Republicans were one vote short. The only vote in question was the vote of Senator Edmund Ross of Kansas. He didn't like Johnson either, but he did not think a president should be impeached for a strictly political reason. Such politicizing would weaken the office of the president. So, on the final vote on May 16, 1868, when Chief Justice Salmon P. Chase asked, "Mr. Ross, how say you?" Senator Ross replied, "Not guilty." Johnson's presidency was saved, but the senator's political career was wrecked. Republicans called Ross a traitor and a beast and a skunk. Voters turned him out of office at the next election.

Years later, even those who lambasted him at the time admitted that he had acted in the best interests of the country. A Kansas newspaper that had once vilified him later concluded, "By the firmness and courage of Senator Ross, the country was saved from calamity greater than war." (Rick Beyer. *The Greatest Presidential Stories Never Told.* New York: Harper Collins, 2007, pp. 84–85)

In the 1960s, Dr. Martin Luther King, Jr. helped organize non-violent civil disobedience by much of the African American community across the South. The back of segregation was eventually broken, but old prejudices did not disappear.

Things are much different today; much good change has taken place. Yet even after the election of Barrack Obama, as our first African American president in 2008, we still have far to go on the road to racial respect and brotherhood from and for all races.

One Easter, when I was four, I got a baby chick, which grew up to be a "mean ole white rooster." One day the rooster got into our pump house kitchen and knocked over and broke Mom's sugar bowl, so Mom rung his neck and fried him for supper.

My parents did not own an automobile (not until the mid-1950s). However, my maternal grandparents, Hugh and Gladys Bishop, had two older automobiles. One was an old faded-green Chevy, which we called the Green Car, the second was a newer blue Nash. We called the Nash, the Blue Car. I was told, once when it would not start, I beat on the grill with a hammer then marched into the house and proudly proclaimed, "I fixed the Blue Car!" I can't remember, but I imagine I "got fixed" for that.

Great Granddad Connelly, with Freddy, in backseat and Clair III in front seat of Dada's Nash, the "Blue Car," in Gainesville, approximately 1943.)

Sometime around 1942/43, we moved to Jay (Santa Rosa County), Florida. Jay was a very small town located about 330 miles west of Gainesville. In Jay, we lived with Grandmom and Granddad Beck (Clair and Edna Beck, Sr.). Granddad was a rural mail carrier for the post office. He owned a Pontiac, which he used to deliver the mail.

Back then, we purchased live chickens at the store. To prepare them for cooking, Grandmom Beck would tie their feet to a clothesline then cut their throat. The chicken would flop around, slinging blood everywhere. Sometimes she would wring their neck instead, then the chicken would run around until it dropped. Then we put the chicken into boiling water to make it easier to pluck the feathers. After singeing the very short feathers over fire, the chicken would be gutted, cleaned, and cut into pieces for frying.

While in Jay, I remember helping carry firewood for the wood-burning cook stove. Once, while carrying an armload of wood to the house, I tripped over a brick and fell. A sharp point on the end of one piece of wood cut me under the chin, nearly down to my throat. I had to be rushed to a hospital in Century, Florida, nine miles away. The doctor medicated me and put several metal clamps in to hold the wound closed. I still carry that scar too.

A few years later, I slipped, while climbing a barbed wire fence, in Gainesville, and cut the front of my right thigh on the barbed wire. It was a nasty open wound the length of my right thigh. I still bear that scar as well.

Normally, going to a doctor, or dentist, was not something poor people did. Money was scarce, and we self-medicated with home remedies. For example, if you stepped on a nail, you put your foot in coal oil (kerosene). If you had pinworms (and most poor people had them) you put a few drops of turpentine on a spoonful of sugar and ate it. I didn't go to a dentist until I was twelve or thirteen and needed a permanent tooth extracted. I was in my late teens when I got my first fillings. I did not go to a dental hygienist until long after my marriage.

February 1944, late into WW II, my dad was drafted, and he requested to be allowed to be inducted in Gainesville, although we lived in Jay. Mom was pregnant with Wayne at that time. (Pic of Dad in uniform.) Thus, we moved back to Gainesville to live with my mom's parents while Dad went through basic training. He was stationed in Jacksonville, Florida (US Navy), for the duration of the war. Having three small children possibly kept the navy from shipping him to a war zone.

During the war, there was a shortage of food staples, and things like rubber, gasoline, and metals. Most of those were taken up by the war effort. What staples and materials that were available for purchase were rationed out. So, the purchase of a bag of sugar had to be accompanied by a rationing stamp. Being able to buy a bag of sugar was a thing to rejoice over. People ran their tires until they were slick and threadbare, because they couldn't buy new ones. All 1943 "one cent" coins, commonly referred to as pennies, were made out of steel. Copper was reserved for the war effort. (Picture of Mom, Clair III, and Wayne [in arms] standing in front of our low-rent housing, Jacksonville, Florida.)

Sometime after Wayne was born, June 5, 1944, we moved to Jacksonville and lived in a low-rent housing project in order to be with Dad. We had a gas refrigerator. *One night, we all nearly suffocated when the pilot light on the gas refrigerator went out and gas continued to flow, filling the apartment with vapors.* Wayne was still a baby; he woke up crying, and the family was able to wake up and get out of the house safely.

In September 1944, I entered first grade at Fishweir Elementary School. There were no kindergartens then. In 2002, my cousin, Nita (Ivey) Tamplin, told me that Fishweir School was still used.

Two phenomenal social changes happened because of the war. First, since so many men were fighting the war, women were hired for factory jobs previously performed only by men. After the war, women remained in the workforce. Prior to that, most women stayed in the home; that was the career of most women.

Second, after being sent around the world to fight the war, the men returned home to become more mobile. Families began to move away from their roots to find jobs in the city. The great urban shift had begun. A popular song of the day asked, "How are you going to keep them down on the farm, after they've seen Paree [Paris]?" As a result of this phenomenon, multiple generations of families living in the same town have almost become a relic of the past.

In January 1945, Franklin D. Roosevelt was inaugurated for his fourth term as president of our country. However, Roosevelt's health deteriorated quickly, and he died in office a few months later, on

April 12, 1945. WW II was still going on but ended a few months later. Vice President Harry Truman, became our thirty-third president. During Truman's presidency, our constitution was amended to limit a president to two terms. *In my opinion, the only thing wrong with that amendment is that we didn't also include term limits for Congress, as well. Please forgive my political bias.*

In 1945, after the war (WW II) ended, we moved back to Gainesville, for a while, before returning to Jay, Florida, where my Beck grandparents lived. In Jay, my dad worked as a carpenter. He also served as unpaid mayor of Jay (population less than five hundred). Later, he ran for election to the school board (paid position) but was defeated. I attended grades 2 through 4 in Jay.

Mom and Dad supplemented their meager income by building and operating a photo booth. They operated it on Saturdays, when lots of people from the outlaying rural areas came to town. Mom would peek into the photo booth to snap the pictures. Dad worked inside the dark room developing and drying the strip of pictures. Mom also made popcorn balls to sell at the photo booth.

I was once referred to as a "German" by some adults in Jay. They knew who I was, but I didn't know them. WW II had just ended, and Germans were not popular. At this writing, I am not positive, but assume I am a descendant of German Becks, not British Becks. I thought that Granddad said that he didn't know. However, Aunt Eleanor told me that her dad said that he was of German heritage.

I am ashamed to admit that I was an adult before I became aware of our country's shameful treatment of Japanese Americans during WW II. They were rounded up like cattle and placed in concentration camps even though they were loyal Americans. We did not trust them.

Several Memories of Jay, Florida:

- Picking blackberries during the summer. Mom often served them with cream at supper. She also canned many jars of blackberry jelly to use throughout the year.

- Playing outdoors until dark, with neighborhood kids (bare-footed all summer).
- Christmas was a wonderful time. We were poor, but we always got one of Dad's socks filled with fruit, nuts, and unwrapped hard candy. We also got at least one nice gift. Once, I got a Lincoln Log set, another year a Tinker Toy Set, another an Erector Set.
- One of my favorite pastimes at school, in Jay, was spinning tops during recess and lunchtime. I also picked the seeds out of pine cones for a small snack. Some called us "poor white trash." Poor we were, but trash we were not.

During the years immediately after WW II, electricity came to the rural areas, through the government program of REA (Rural Electrification Administration). The government built a lot of dams along rivers in order to generate electricity. One well-known project was the TVA (Tennessee Valley Authority). It was good to trade in kerosene lanterns for electric lightbulbs and "ice boxes" for refrigerators. However, we still used "ice boxes" for many more years. The dams formed large lakes, which became recreation areas after the economy improved. *Round Mountain, Alabama, where my dad lived while attending high school across the river, in Center City, Alabama, is at the bottom of one of those lakes.*

Our small two-bedroom rented house in Jay had an enclosed flush toilet on the covered back porch. We took spit baths every day (washed our face and feet in the sink). We usually took a tub bath on Saturday night. We used a number 2 washtub, which we placed on the floor of the kitchen. I remember Dad sat in one tub and put his feet in another tub. Mom heated bathwater on the kerosene kitchen stove.

One sad event happened while Mom was heating water for something. A younger cousin, Jerry Dauphinee, visiting from Gainesville, sat down on the open oven door and tipped the kerosene cook stove over. The boiling water flew over his head and scalded my mom's legs. Mom stayed in bed several weeks, with her legs propped up. Fortunately, Jerry was hardly burned.

In the early summer, I "hoed cotton" (weeded the fields with a long handle hoe). In late summer, I "picked cotton" (we did not pull off the cotton bolls, like today). I was only eight and not very good at it, so my earnings were meager. I still remember how hot the ground was between the rows of cotton. I would stand in the shade of the cotton plants so my bare feet would not get hot.

I walked to school, in Jay. It was just over a mile, but it seemed such a long distance, especially in the winter or when it rained. My parents did not have a vehicle. In fact, my parents bought their first automobile in 1954, six years after moving to Texas. It was a nearly new, demonstration vehicle, a 1954 Mercury, four-door sedan. I didn't even own a bicycle until I was twelve, a gift from grandmother.

We were lucky to have one good pair of shoes. We wore them until they "wore out." We got holes in the soles before the tops wore out. No problem, we cut a piece of cardboard and put it inside the shoe. Presto—no more hole. Two new problems: you had to replace the cardboard every day, and on rainy days, the water penetrated the cardboard, and your sock got wet and muddy.

Our family continued to expand, a fourth kid, then another on the way. My sisters, Sharon (July 21, 1946) and Brenda (October 24, 1947), were born while we were in Jay. However, Mom went to the hospital in Brewton, Alabama (fifteen miles north of Jay), to give birth to each of them. I remember Mom telling me that she had one or two (?) miscarriages, but I don't know when that was.

We moved to a new and larger wood-frame rent house about two blocks away. A few months later, Mom's sister Dot and her husband, Fred, and their first child, Sandra, moved to Jay. They rented a wood-frame house a block away. They even hooked up a telephone. I was impressed. However, Uncle Fred couldn't find suitable work, so they moved away a few months later.

Our new rent house did not have a flush toilet. Instead, we walked down a path behind the house to a wooden outhouse. It was some years before I learned that you could actually buy things from the Sears & Roebuck catalog. Until then, I thought the catalog was meant to entertain you, until time to tear out a page with which to wipe yourself. The catalog also helped me keep my mind off "the thought of falling into the cesspool."

I remember how proud I was on the day I traded my sling shot for a Daisy "Red Rider" BB gun. Actually, I did not give up the slingshot, I just stuffed it in the back pocket of my overalls. My parents never allowed me to use the more common racial slur slang word for a slingshot. I am happy that they taught me better.

Such were the "good ole days." Yet good days they were. We were happy with less because we knew of nothing else. We were never bored, because we learned to make up our own games, create our own toys from paper, cardboard, sticks, or wood. During the long hot summers, we played outside with neighborhood kids until dark. We had everything we really needed.

Another highlight of our time in Jay was meeting Earl Braunhardt, the fiancé of Dad's youngest sister, Doris. I attended their wedding in Milton, Florida. "Uncle Brownie" was in the navy and played trombone in the military base band. I remember him taking me to a football game at the base. I was allowed to sit in the bleachers with the band. Too bad music is not learned by osmosis.

My first remembrance of spiritual things was in Jay. I attended Sunday school at First Baptist. Mom and Dad were active, and Dad was a deacon. I can remember my Mom baking unleavened flat bread to use in the Lord's Supper. I was in RAs (Royal Ambassadors) a missions education organization for young boys, then led by the WMU. During that time, I was witnessed to and I made some favorable indication about faith in Christ. However, I did not understand much. One morning in Sunday school, I and others were encouraged to make public professions of faith in Christ and be baptized that evening. However, I did not return that evening. I remember being afraid and confused. Actually, I don't think that we children normally attended evening services anyway.

I do remember sneaking to church one Sunday evening to hear my mom and dad sing a duet. I was babysitting my brothers and sisters at home but left them alone and ran to church (about half a mile). I listened from outside the building as Mom and Dad sang then ran home. I never told them what I did. I should not have left my younger siblings alone.

The worse sunburn I ever suffered (actually all the family got burned) was on a swimming trip to Fort Walton Beach, Florida. We were all seriously burned.

The family moved back to Gainesville, early in the summer of 1948. I went reluctantly because I, at nine, was "in love" with May Carol somebody, the daughter of the local telephone operator. That was before dial phones and all calls, local as well as long distance, had to be placed through an operator. Few people had phones, and most of those who did had a party line (shared line). Thus, you could listen in on other people's conversations.

Mom and Dad never had a telephone until after we moved to Texas. Dad was serving as mayor of Jay when we moved away. I can remember the "going-away party." Mom and Dad were given a radio with a wooden case, about the size of three large shoeboxes.

Dada Bishop drove a truck from the moss factory in Gainesville and moved us back to Gainesville. In Gainesville, we again lived in Mom's parents' barn. Actually, Dada and Mama had divorced a couple of years before that. I still remember Dada and Mama telling the family they would part. I did not understand divorce then but remember my mom and her sisters cried.

October 1948: Left Florida, Moved to Texas (Age 10 through College)

Sometime after we arrived back in Gainesville, in 1948, Mama (Grandmother Bishop) went to Texas with a friend. She met Woody and Jo Ellen Walker, who were building a dream house. Mama arranged for Dad to work on Mr. Walker's home. So Dad went to Galveston, Texas, to work. After a few months, he wired money and sent word for Mom and us kids to come.

Late October 1948, I moved to Galveston, Texas, on a Greyhound bus with Mother and my four siblings. Our belongings were carried in cardboard boxes. Brenda was only a year old. Clair and I were each given a roll of pennies to spend along the way. Wayne, Sharon, and Brenda were too young to know what to do with money (how things have changed for kids today). At every bus station along the way, Clair and I hit the gum machines (one cent).

After living in two different low-rent beachfront motels for a few weeks, we moved into a three-bedroom ground-floor apartment in a low-rent, government housing project (68-H Oleander Addition), at the north end of Fifty-first Street.

The whole family attended church together, when we first moved to Galveston. First Baptist hired a bus, from the city bus company, to pick people up and take them to Sunday school and then back home after morning

worship. One Sunday, my brother, Clair, made a public decision for Christ. I knew about Jesus and I went forward too, but my decision was not based on knowledge. *Clair and I were baptized that evening, but I did not become a true follower of Jesus until I was fifteen.*

I learned to swim in Galveston, at age eleven or twelve. But I have always had a healthy respect (or is it an unhealthy fear?) of water. At age nine, in Jay, Florida, I was in danger of drowning twice on the same day. I was with some older boys swimming in the Escambia River between Jay and Century. I was swept downstream, but some of the older boys were able to reach me and pull me out. Later that day, we swam in a nearby lake. I was holding on the back of a wooden rowboat. Thinking we had come back to shallow water, I turned loose of the boat and proceeded to sink; they pulled me out again.

I enjoyed swimming at the beach at Galveston but did not go in over my head. I did swim in deep water in Offet's Bayou in Galveston. I also did some water skiing there. A friend in high school had a 25-horse power Evenrude outboard motor and a pair of wide wooden water skies. He and I and two other buddies (Ben and Efraim Armendariz) would rent an aluminum fishing boat, attach the motor, and ski in the bayou. No one today would believe that you could water ski that way, but we did.

As a missionary, I enjoyed body surfing in the Indonesian/Indian Ocean with fellow missionaries and our families. The surf was very rough, but the water was clear, and it was great for body surfing. However, I do not enjoy swimming and rarely do; sad because Linda loves swimming.

Mom was the cement that held the family together. She was a good seamstress, cook, and was also the chief love giver. She was practical, frugal, and dependent on God, thereby enabling us to survive on a limited income without any outside aide.

Dad was a hard worker but did not always have a job. He was very intelligent on a broad array of subjects. My brother Clair, and my sister Sharon are also very smart, and they did well in school.

I was not a very good student, especially throughout my public school career. I especially had problems with math, English, and spelling. They didn't seem to know much about learning disabilities back then, but that is what I had. I thought I was dumb and did not have much self-esteem. I hated school, except for lunch, recess, and being with friends. Later, I witnessed two of my own children struggle with school because of similar learning difficulties.

Even today, students like us still fall through the cracks. Education systems "seem" to be created for students who learn easily. People like me can learn, but the system often attempts to force us to learn the same way as the so-called "good or normal students" learn. We can't do that, however; we can often excel too, if an education system/teacher learns to appreciate how we learn and then facilitates that learning process. Even today, one of my granddaughters recently encountered this in university.

I met my first Mexican Americans at Alamo Elementary School in Galveston. Many of the Anglo boys said bad things about them, so at first, I didn't become friends with any of the Mexican kids. However, later, when I played baseball, several Mexican boys were on my team; they were nice guys and most were good players.

In junior high school, I met the Armanderiz family. Ben and Efraim became my best friends, and I loved their family. After that, I had several Hispanic friends. Ben and Efraim were both in our wedding. Ben was my best man, and Efraim was one of two groomsmen. David Arnold was my other groomsman. David had been a classmate too; he was also a son of my favorite Sunday school teacher. Verna Moreno, one of Linda's Hispanic friends, was one of her three bride's maids.

In 1956, our housing unit was demolished to make way for a bridge to nearby Pelican Island, where Todd Shipyard was located. We had to move two blocks away, to 36-J Oleander Addition, on Fifty-third street. I attended Alamo Elementary School, Lovenberg Junior High (no longer standing), and graduated from the then new Ball High School, June 1956.

Our Babe Ruth League team was the Galveston City champions both years I played. I had not played organized baseball before that. In fact, I didn't even try out for the team. I watched them practice, and the coach asked me if I wanted to play. I started in "left field," then halfway through the season, I was moved to "first base." The next year I was moved to "shortstop," the best position in baseball, as far as I am concerned.

I played organized baseball as a thirteen- and fourteen-year-old and again when I was seventeen. I wanted to play baseball every year, because I had begun to listen to professional baseball games on the radio and had dreams of being a pro baseball player. My favorite players were Bob Feller, pitcher for the Cleveland Indians, and Ted Williams, outfielder for the Boston Red Sox. I needed to work after school, thus had no time for baseball. I also worked summers help-ing Dad (carpenter). I still loved baseball, but I didn't really have the talent to become a professional. After reading several detective books, I thought I would like to become a "private eye." What would I become when grown?

The family made several trips back to Florida to visit family. Two of those trips were after the deaths of Great-granddaddy Connelly and Great-grandmother (DeLoach) Connelly.

In 1951, at age thirteen, while in junior high, I began my first job for pay ($13 a week). I worked thirty-two hours a week after school and on weekends at the Broadway Theater, Fifty-first and Broadway. I walked to work and back home. I started as parking lot attendant then became an usher. Laws today prevent children under sixteen from working. However, I did not regard my working to be a bad thing then; I still haven't changed my mind.

Beginning at age thirteen, I began buying almost all my own clothes and began giving Mom $5 a week to help with family expenses. Mom did not ask me to do that, but she allowed me to do it. She seemed proud that I wanted to assume some responsibility, plus money was scarce, even with Mom and Dad both working.

In 1954, I also sold Sunday newspapers each Saturday evening at one of the drive-in restaurants on the beach. I earned five cents for every fifteen cents paper I sold. If I didn't sell them all, I took them home and walked throughout my neighborhood, early Sunday morning shouting, "Sunday morning *Houston Post* paper" until all were sold.

After working at the theater nearly four years, I left and began working at the Seawall Cafe, on the seawall facing the Gulf of Mexico. I began as a busboy but became the counter waiter after a few weeks. The tables were waited on by women, most of whom were divorced single moms supporting their children. That was my first understanding of the plight of single, divorced, or widowed mothers.

In the summer of 1955, just before starting my senior year in high school, I took a two-week unpaid vacation, a solo trip back to Florida (via Greyhound Bus) to visit grandparents, aunts and uncles, cousins (and a few old friends who barely remembered me). At that time, I still hoped to be able to return to Florida, after high school, to live with my grandmother and attend the University of Florida. We had lived in Texas for seven years, but I still regarded Florida to be home. I still had "sand in my shoes" (a Florida saying for people coming to Florida and staying).

Although I had been sweet on a few girls off and on, I was very bashful and was a sophomore in high school before I had my first real girlfriend. Jo Verne lived in a second-floor apartment in the building directly behind us. She was a drum majorette at Lovenburg Junior High. Our first date was a "hay ride" given by her church (Methodist). Her father was one of the chaperons. We were very thick for many months, but alas, only "puppy love." Jo Verne never spoke to me again after we broke up.

Later, I dated Sue Ann for a short time. She was a Ball High School majorette and a member of my church. After a football game date, I tried to kiss her, but she wouldn't let me. Later, I learned that she was actually "in love with a sailor." We remained friends but did not date again.

Thus I had very little dating experience when I met Linda Rountree, in early 1956. I was a senior at Ball High; Linda was a sophomore. I had known Linda's name for several years because she was a friend of Dinah Armendariz, the younger sister of my two best friends, Ben and Ephraim. Their father, Rev. G. M. Armendariz, was pastor of the First Mexican Presbyterian Church of Galveston.

At first, I was not interested in dating Linda. Oh, she was a very pretty young lass, but my intention was to torment her boyfriend. I don't remember why I disliked Dale. I think it began with a problem in ROTC; I can't remember. I washed dishes in the school cafeteria, during lunchtime, for a hot lunch. I saw Dale with this pretty young lady every day, so I started flirting with her in front of him. Each day, at lunch, I would go over to their table to talk to Linda while ignoring Dale. Later, I started calling her on the phone every afternoon, at Dale's normal time to call. I did everything I could think of to torment the guy and break them up.

Well, I finally succeeded, but in the process, I fell into my own trap. I fell hard for Linda myself. I am thankful my hatefulness to Dale did not turn her against me. I started getting invitations to birthday parties from her friends. Finally, I asked her for a real date. However, my dad did not get home with the car, so I had to call Linda and break that first date—real impressive! But, a few months later, we started "going steady" (exclusive dating). She wore my senior class ring on a necklace chain.

After graduation from high school (June 1956), I got a full-time job reading light meters with the Houston Lighting and Power Company in Galveston. After reading light meters for about seven months, I was promoted to an inside clerical job. I remained at that job until

I left, in January 1958, to enter Howard Payne College (now HP University).

I proposed to Linda in July 1956, just over a month before her 16th birthday. Linda helped me pick out her engagement and wedding rings, and I bought them at Zale's Jewelry. She wore her engagement ring on dates for a month, but took it off before she got home. I officially gave her the ring on her sixteenth birthday; after that, she wore it all the time. Of course, I asked Mr. Rountree for Linda's hand in marriage. Mr. and Mrs. Rountree were not very happy about their young daughter being engaged, but were nice.

Well, they were nice to me, but they gave Linda a hard time over the engagement. They lightened up later; they probably thought we would change our minds along the way. I turned eighteen a week prior to officially giving Linda her engagement ring on her sixteenth birthday.

From time to time, Linda and I purchased items that we would need when married. We also received many nice gifts when we married, June 6, 1959.

My friend Efraim Armendariz and I joined the Marine Reserves in the spring of 1956. The best I remember, Efraim's older brother, Joshua, talked us into joining his unit. Joshua had formerly served in the navy and had an honorable discharge.

In 1956, I did summer training with the Marine Corps, in Hawthorne, Nevada. During our training, the Suez Canal crisis broke out, and we were nearly sent to the Suez Canal. In 1957, our training was in San Diego, California. During that time, the Lebanon crisis arose, and we were almost shipped out to Lebanon. I received an honorable discharge in May 1962.

Other than those two crises, the closest I came to a war zone were the night war games we participated in during each summer, during training. One amusing event took place during our summer in and around San Diego. Someone stole our company banner, which flew outside our company headquarters. The company camped down the road was suspect. Our captain offered a weekend pass for whoever was able to bring our banner home.

Efraim and I went out to look for it. Although we didn't find our banner, we come upon one of the guys from the suspect company. He picked a quiet location, some distance from his unit, to relieve himself. We drew down on him, took his weapon (unloaded, like ours), and took him captive. Our captain traded our captive for our banner. Efraim and I received our weekend passes and visited my family, then living in Los Angeles.

Fred Becomes Self-Dependent

*M*eanwhile, in the fall of 1956, Dad went to California to find work, after a friend wrote him about a job there.

In January 1957, I drove Mom and my siblings to California, in the family car (1954 Mercury), with the family belongings crammed into a medium-sized open U-Haul trailer.

After a few days in California, I returned to work in Galveston via Greyhound Bus Lines. I did not move to California with the family because I was engaged to Linda. I also planned to attend Howard Payne College in Brownwood, Texas, in the near future.

I rented a bedroom (with kitchen privileges) from an elderly widow, Mrs. Lloyd (Momma Lloyd), an older friend of Mrs. Rountree. Momma. Lloyd lived a half mile from downtown where I worked, so I walked to work. But a few months later, she moved several miles away, so I rode the public bus to work. In late summer 1957, while working at HL&P Co., I purchased my first car, a 1947 Studebaker coupe, for $125. It used a lot of oil and often had to be pushed to get it started. I sold it for the same amount, when leaving for college, several months later.

In the summer of 1957, I had my first paid vacation (one week). During that time, FBC was conducting a youth-led revival with a preacher and a singer/music leader team from Southwestern Baptist Seminary. Because of my vacation, I was able to make evangelistic visits with the song leader and, during that week, felt God's call into full-time ministry. I did not understand all the ramifications of God's call, but God's word says we are to walk by faith, not by sight. I have never questioned God's call or my decision to follow His call.

I preached my first sermon, at my home church (FBC Galveston) on Wednesday evening before Thanksgiving 1957. After that, Richard Steele, a young pastor at Port Bolivar, gave me my second opportunity. Twelve years later, Richard and his wife were in missionary orientation with us in the fall of 1969. They served in Mexico for several years.

My pastor, Dr. John Salzmann, became an encourager to me. He periodically gave me assignments to visit shut-ins (elderly men and women no longer physically able to attend worship services). My church also licensed/endorsed me to preach the Gospel.

Several deacons also took me under their wing and invited me to join them on their Saturday morning breakfast/prayer meeting in a restaurant. They and their wives often invited Linda and me to join a small group of them after Sunday evening worship for a meal and fellowship at some café.

Linda and I attended the Deaf Training Union Class on Sunday evenings. We made some progress in signing and reading sign language, but later we dropped out to do something else. We lost most of what we had learned ... a regret.

Howard Payne College, Brownwood, Texas

*I*n January 1958, I resigned my job with HL&P Co and moved, by bus, to Brownwood, Texas, to enroll in Howard Payne College (now university). HPC was a small (1,200 students) accredited liberal arts Baptist College. *Upon arrival, I had to take an entrance exam, before I could register, because my high school grades, though passing, were very low. I arrived at HPC with nearly $200 in my pocket and all my earthly belongs in a footlocker and a suitcase.* Although my parents were not able to help me financially, they had prepared me to make it on my own. I could cook, wash, and iron my clothes; earn a salary; manage my meager cash; etc. I had already completely supported myself for a year prior to entering college.

Howard Payne was a great school for me. They gave admission to me even though I had poor high school grades and had very little money. They gave me a job working on the campus labor crew (cleaning buildings, mowing grass, plumbing repairs, etc.) for fifty cents an hour, or about $40/month. Actually, I received no money; it was all applied to my school and dormitory fees. Because I was ministerial student, The Baptist General Convention of Texas paid half of my tuition.

Occasionally, I was able to pick up an odd job here and there, which provided a little cash for toiletries and other personal needs. The tuition was $12 per semester hour, plus room and board, books, and other fees. Later tuition was raised by 50 percent to $18. That sounds cheap now, but it was expensive in that economy.

God provided as extra needs arose. Later, after Linda and I married, Mom Rountree talked with a friend, who was a member of Eastern Stars. Her friend then sponsored efforts to get an Estaral Religious Scholarship for me. She was successful, and the scholarship provided $500 each semester for the 1960–61 school year. I was awarded a second year, but completed my college studies in January 1962, so was only able to use the second scholarship for one semester.

At HPC, before marriage, I was active in Life Service Band, which conducted weekend revivals in country churches all around central Texas. *My favorite professor and one of the most influential people in my spiritual life was Dr. Nat Tracy, in the Department of Religion.*

I made a few trips to Galveston to see Linda. I got rides (helped pay for gasoline) with fellow students, who lived in Houston area, then hitchhiked on to Galveston (fifty miles).

In Brownwood, I was a member of Ave. D Baptist Church and taught an adult Bible class. For a while, I led the music and directed the choir, even though I could neither read music, nor carry a tune. In reality, Mrs. Bourganier, the pianist, was the real director.

One Saturday, while preaching on the street, with fellow students, I began to realize that *I had been baptized at age ten, before I actually became a true follower of Jesus. My real conversion took place five years later, at age fifteen. So I asked Ave. D to baptize me as a true believer.* I believe that baptism has no role in our salvation. However, believers' baptism is important as a public identification with Jesus, in obedience to Him.

Baptism is also an outward symbol and testimony of something that has happened inside a person who follows Jesus (a death to sin and new life in and through Christ, as well as a faith in the resurrection). Thus, although I have been immersed twice in a Baptist church, I have only been baptized once as a believer.

In June 1958, I took a Greyhound Bus to California to work, during the summer break, in the receiving department at Ramo-Wooldridge (now TRW). During that time, I lived with my parents and four siblings, in the small three-bedroom, one-bath, (1,200 sq. ft.) home my parents had purchased. in Redondo Beach.

In late August 1958, I returned to Texas and, after visiting Linda, in Galveston, returned to Howard Payne in Brownwood. *It is ironic, but during my summer in California, I finally became a Texan. I lost the sand from my shoes and no longer wanted to return to Florida.* It seemed that I had always lived in the past instead of the present, looking backward instead of forward, in regard to feeling at home. No more!

The move to California was good for my parents. They worked hard and were able to move from "poverty" to the ranks of "lower middle class" and purchased their first and only home together.

Marriage—June 6, 1959

I n late May 1959, I drove to Galveston in the used 1953 Chevy purchased in Brownwood. Linda and I pooled much of our meager savings to make a down payment on our first car.

Galveston, Saturday, June 6, 1959. (Rear) Reverend John W. Salzman. (Main row L-R), Verna Moreno, Marilyn Day, Joyce Sharp, Linda & Fred, Ben Armendariz, Efraim Armendariz, David Arnold. (Children L-R), Betsy Sharp, Crissie Dee Richmond, Randy Holland

Mom was able to fly in from California, but Dad was unable to attend (high price of flying, plus he needed to stay home with my four younger siblings). At that time, for a young man to marry, he had to either be twenty-one years old, or have a notarized written permission from his parents. I was only twenty. Young women could marry without parental permission, if they were eighteen. Linda was already eighteen.

After a very brief honeymoon in Houston, Texas, we moved to Brownwood, because a summer job with HL&P did not materialize. *Thankfully, Mr. George Collier Sr., a member at FBC Galveston and the chief engineer of the Gulf Colorado and Santa Fe Railroad, arranged a summer job for me in Brownwood, where they were constructing a new switching yard.* His son, George Jr., was my classmate at BHS, and Bruce Collier was a classmate of Linda's. The salary was $2 per hour, which was very good.

However, *en route to Brownwood pulling a small U-Haul trailer, we broke down, and our car's engine had to be overhauled.* Three days later, Linda and I finally arrived in Brownwood, with less than $200 after paying for the engine overhaul and travel expenses.

Rev. Lavoid and Geneva Robertson, my pastor at Ave. D Baptist Church, took us in for the night. The next day (Thursday), we located a furnished garage apartment and moved in. However, it was too late to buy any groceries. Back then, grocery stores were all closed by 6:00 or 7:00 PM. There were no stores that stayed open twenty-four hours/day.

I began my job with the railroad the next morning (Friday), without breakfast. I was so hot, tired, and hungry that first day. I thought they had worked us right through lunch. So when the "water man" came by again (everyone drank from the same dipper from the water carried in a steel pail), I asked him what time it was. He pulled out his pocket watch and said, "Ten a.m." Well, lunchtime eventually came, and I drove over to a café and got a hamburger and Coca-Cola.

That first day was pretty difficult. I returned home to Linda exhausted, sore, and burned by the creosote on the RR ties. The weekend saved me, because it gave me time to "lick my wounds," rest up (and for Linda to build up my spirits), therefore I was able to return to work Monday morning.

I was finally able to work on a spiking team, driving railroad spikes in creosoted wooden railroad ties to hold the steel rails in place. However, I was pretty slow. I worked with a nice older Hispanic man without many teeth. We stood across the rail from each other and drove the same spike with alternating strikes, with our long-handled spiking maul (hammer). He never looked up but chuckled in a singsong voice, *"Hitty one, missy two, hitty one, missy two."* He was describing my lack of proficiency at driving spikes.

Later that fall, while serving as chainman on the engineering team, I had to drive two-by-two stakes (elevation stakes) into the ground with a long-handled sledgehammer. *I often over-swung the stake with the sledge hammer*, which meant I hit the stake with the handle of the sledge hammer. That resulted in a broken handle. I went through a lot of handles. *I didn't have a very high batting average when I played baseball either.*

At summer's end, as I prepared to quit my job and return to college, the engineering team offered me a job as chainman on their four-man team. Since the job was due to be completed in January 1960, it meant that I would only need to drop out of college for the 1959 fall semester. Mr. Collier was probably behind that job as well, for I was not a qualified engineer. I believe it was God who opened that opportunity, for we really needed the money.

My pay on the engineering team was much better (about $400 per month, plus expenses). Since the engineering team was based in Galveston, the members received a rent allowance and a per diem toward food while in Brownwood. *Linda and I were able to live on my expense check and save most of my paycheck. Thus, in January 1960, when I left the railroad, we were able to pay cash for furniture and appliances to fill the small efficiency apartment* in the HPC ministerial court and savings toward the next semester.

I returned to school and to part-time work with the HPC campus maintenance crew (back to fifty cents an hour). I also worked two hours weekday evenings and Saturday mornings for cash, at the Coca-Cola plant. I unloaded and reloaded trucks for the next day's route.

Linda gave birth to our first child, Pamela Ann, on May 5, 1960, in Brownwood. We had no health insurance, but fortunately, Linda was still carried on her parents' policy. Linda's mom and dad drove up to Brownwood, from Galveston, to help out after Linda and Pam came home from the hospital.

*We drove our nonair-conditioned 1953 Chevy to California, during the summer of 1960. We wanted to show off our beautiful daughter to my parents. I was their firstborn child. Pam was their firstborn grandchild. They were as proud of her as we were. The same could be said of Mom and Dad Rountree.

I was called as pastor of the Energy Baptist Church, Energy, Texas. I also continued to work my campus crew job. EBC was a small rural halftime church. They had Sunday school every week, but preaching only on the first and third Sunday each month. The people at Energy Baptist Church were good to us. They were a rural church without much hope of growing, for the community was in decline. As young people married, most of them moved to larger towns to make a living. The church felt its main purpose was to help train young preachers.

We often spent the weekend with some of the members. We enjoyed them, and we learned a lot. Many funny things happened while I was pastor in Energy. Linda had never been in the country, so they got a lot of laughs from the "city girl." The funniest thing, in my memory, happened one Sunday morning while making the one-hour drive to Energy. We were over halfway to church when I reached over to give Pam a love tap on the bottom, only to discover her bottom was bare. Linda reached to the back seat to fetch the diaper bag, and it was not in the car. We had to return to Brownwood to get it. Needless to say, we were a bit late for Sunday school that day. The people laughed about that; we still do.

During those days, the "infant seat," the precursor to the modern-day car seat, was invented. It was a simple L-shaped plastic seat, with a removable plastic pad. It doubled as a type of bed. It was light and easy to carry in your arms (no handle). It was not meant to be a safety seat; cars didn't even have seat belts then. People at Energy got a kick out of it and referred to it as a corn scoop.

Energy Baptist issued an annual call to their pastor. Thus I was reelected as pastor each August. However, in August of 1961, the church knew I would graduate the following January and would need to move away to attend seminary. Perhaps, they felt it best to go ahead and call a new pastor in August 1961 rather than having no pastor from January 1962 until August 1962. Wow, the power of traditions. That was a blow that caused me much agony.

I felt that it seemed expedient to the members. I know they loved us, and had they realized how devastating it would be to me, I feel sure that they would have waited until I left to call a new pastor, perhaps even before the traditional August call. *Yes, it hurt, but I got over it. My fond memories of Energy were not discolored.*

With our second baby on the way, we needed more income, so I got a job (4:00 p.m.–midnight) with Lampkin Brother's Feed Mill. It was a horrible, dirty job, but pay on the swing shift was $1.15/hour. I continued full-time studies at HPC.

Our second child, Stephen Wayne, was born in Brownwood, on October 26, 1961. This was no ordinary birth. Linda was barely seven months pregnant when she had an appendicitis attack one evening while I was still at work. There was no choice; her appendix had to be removed that night. The next day, Steve was born, by natural birth. He arrived two months early and weighed only four pounds.

Linda became very ill after Steve's birth and nearly died. God's mercy and the help of Mrs. Mary Ann Matthews, a nurse, who volunteered a second shift at no cost after working her regular shift (midnight–8:00 a.m.). *Mrs. Matthews kept turning Linda from side to side to help get rid of the poisons that were in her system. That played an important part in saving her life. Grace again.* We met Mrs. Matthews and her family right after moving to Brownwood. They rented the house in front of the garage apartment we rented, while working on the railroad. Her oldest daughter was married just before us and moved from Brownwood. So, Mrs. Matthews sort of adopted us.

HPC Graduation and Move to California

In January 1962, I completed my bachelor of arts, with a major in Bible and a minor in history. *That I was able to complete my studies in four calendar years was amazing. I had not gone to college one fall semester (while with the railroad) during those four years. I was able to catch up through two summers of summer school and by taking eighteen units some semesters.*

It was even more remarkable that I was able to bring my four-year grade point average up to a B during my last semester. No less remarkable was the fact that I arrived at HPC single and left with a wife, two children, and a lot of varied work experiences.

At that time, HPC only had graduation ceremonies in May and in August. It was too costly for me to travel back to Texas from California. Thus, I was not able to return for my graduation ceremony, so was awarded the BA, "in absentia."

I planned to enroll in Golden Gate Baptist Theological Seminary, but first, I needed to work to pay off a few hundred dollars in college debts. So, we decided to go to Redondo Beach, California, where my parents were and look for a job.

My brother Clair was married with one son, Chris. He volunteered to take off from work and drove to Texas to pull a trailer to California for us. My brother Wayne traveled with him. Our '53 Chevy barely made the trip to California; it would not have been able to pull the trailer (about twelve feet long). Clair had an Oldsmobile '88, it was old too, but much better than our car.

Clair and Wayne were most gracious, and their help proved to be indispensable. Both of my brothers continue to help people, but

Clair has been especially unselfish. He has helped many people, even to the detriment of his own needs and plans.

We lived with my mom and dad for several weeks, until I could get a job and rent an apartment. Shortly after we arrived and before getting a job, Steve got very sick with pneumonia. We had no hospitalization. Mom's doctor, Dr. Hallesey, took pity on us and arranged for oxygen, etc., to be delivered to the house. He also made house calls—something he didn't normally do. Of course, I see it, like Mrs. Matthews's help after Steve's birth, as God's continued provision. After all, one of His names, is Jehovah Jireh (God Himself is our provision).

I was able to get a job in the receiving department at Space Technology Labs (STL) a spinoff from Ramo-Wooldridge.

We had met Diane, Clair's wife, before they were married. She made a trip to Florida with Mom and Dad, Clair, Wayne, Sharon, and Brenda. They stopped in Brownwood to visit us. Diane was a big help arranging for us to get an apartment, conveniently next door to them.

The eighteen months we lived in Redondo Beach, between college and seminary, were good. It gave Linda opportunity to solidify her relationship with my parents and siblings. We enjoyed living next door to Clair and Diane. We also met and began relationships with Naomi, Mike, and Steve, the future spouses of my younger siblings, Wayne, Sharon, and Brenda.

I had the privilege of performing the wedding of those three siblings. During that time, Linda and I established an adult relationship with my younger siblings. We even became youth leaders at church for Sharon and Brenda and their friends. We were also able to pay off my college debt during that period.

It was nice to be close to my family, but of course, we were now much farther away from Mom and Dad Rountree, in Texas. They drove out for a visit that summer, and we took in the sights at Sequoia National Park, where we enjoyed nature. We rented a cabin and listened to the bears raid garbage cans at night.

Our third child, Micah Lynn, was born in Redondo Beach, on November 23, 1962, the day after Thanksgiving.

My Grandmother Beck died in 1962, just after Christmas. Mom and Dad planned to drive to Jay, Florida, for her funeral, so I took off of work and helped them drive. Dad had a Buick special (compact sedan); my two sisters, Sharon and Brenda, also went. We picked up Dad's sister Betty in Phoenix, Arizona. She flew in from Salt Lake City. Thus, the six of us were like sardines in a can.

Granddad Beck purchased a brick house in Jay, about a year prior to Grandmother's death. That was the first home they ever owned. As a young boy, I had a slight fear of Granddad Beck. He was quiet, and I don't remember him smiling much. My memory is probably flawed, for in later life, he often smiled. I really enjoyed Granddad after I became old enough to get to know and appreciate him. But soon after that, we went overseas and seldom got to visit him.

While living in Southern California, Linda and I joined FBC of Hermosa Beach, California. and learned a lot, when a few months after our arrival, the church dismissed their pastor. Somehow, we managed to maintain a close relationship with both factions in the church. The people were good to us. After eighteen months, when we prepared to move to the San Francisco Bay Area to attend Golden Gate Seminary, the church voted to ordain me.

A few months after moving to California, a remarkable thing happened. I felt at home in California. Since then, I have always looked forward, instead of backward. That has been a wonderful transformation and keeps me in the "present" instead of in the "past."

Golden Gate Seminary, Mill Valley, California

I resigned my job at STL, in early August 1963, to give us time to make a trip to Galveston, to visit Mom and Dad Rountree. We also continued on to Florida to visit my Bishop grandparents in Gainesville and Granddad Beck in Jay, because none of them had met Linda. While in Jay, I painted the trim on Granddad's house. Several months prior to that trip, we traded in the '53 Chevy and purchased a used 1961 Corvair (a small four-door, rear-engine Chevy). On the way home to California, we again stopped in Galveston. Mom Rountree decided to travel back to California with us to help with our move to Northern California.

FBC Hermosa gave us a good sendoff for our move to Mill Valley, CA to begin seminary. Many people told me that I had so much faith, to quit my job and move my family to a strange place and enroll in school.

I guess I believed them, but after beginning my studies, I was unable to find work to support the family. Then, I began to panic (so much for that great faith), so I wrote Granddad Beck and asked him to loan me $200, which he did. But before I could repay him, Aunt Eleanor, my dad's sister, paid the debt for me. She did so as an offering to God. She also wanted

to invest in me. Many years later, I was able to give her money to pay the first month's rent in a retirement complex.

Golden Gate Seminary was located on beautiful Strawberry Point, in Mill Valley. From the chapel, the city of San Francisco was visible across the bay. The administrators and professors were all very friendly and helpful. I liked all my profs, but my favorite was Dr. Clayton Harrop, Professor of New Testament and Greek.

Soon after being humbled by discovering that my faith was not so great after all, the Lord provided a job. I passed the civil service exam and was hired as a correctional officer (guard) at San Quentin Prison.

During my interview, the interviewers seemed to be concerned with my Southern roots, because they questioned me about racial issues. Finally they asked, "What if a 'black' inmate spit in your face, what would you do?" I had no idea what I would do, nor had I any idea of the answer they "fished for," but answered, "I guess that depends on how big he is." I guess they were satisfied because they just chuckled and asked me no more questions.

San Quentin was the largest prison in the California Department of Corrections; one of the oldest too. After completing a couple of weeks of rotating shifts, to learn the ropes, I settled into the "third watch" (swing shift: 4:00 p.m.–midnight). That enabled me to attend my classes during the morning and early afternoon. The early weeks were the most difficult, because I had to spend them in a gun tower. All new recruits have to experience that. However, after a few weeks, I was assigned duty on the ground, inside the cell blocks. At first, that was a bit scary, especially at night, but there was nothing to be afraid of as long as you stayed alert.

The four cell blocks (west, south, east, and north blocks) were connected at their corners and formed the likeness of walls of a large fortress, with a large somewhat open area in the middle of the four cell blocks. That somewhat square area, contained two adjoining dining halls and the kitchen. There was also a main, paved upper prison yard.

One night, while patrolling the fifth tier (story), in the south block (the largest cell block with a maximum capacity of two thousand inmates), an inmate that I had not met called to me as I passed by his cell. "Mister Beck! They tell me that you are studying to become a minister."

"Yes," I replied. "That is correct." *Then he asked, "With you being a preacher, how do you justify working here and keeping me locked up in this 'hellhole'?"*

I thought a moment, then smiled and responded, "I have a wife and three children that I must provide for. Besides, not many of our correctional officers are Christians. Would you rather we Christian officers quit and leave you to the non-Christian officers?" He was quiet for a moment, then smiled and said, "No, you should stay."

Perhaps due to my Marine Corps training, I tried to dress sharp. My uniform was always in tiptop shape and fit well. I always spit-shined my boots. I expected the inmates to obey the prison rules, but I did not hassle them. I treated them with respect, and they respected me in return.

Eventually, I was assigned as "night yard officer," one of the choice jobs on my shift. Later, I landed the best job on my watch: "kitchen officer." During the eighteen months that I worked in the kitchen, there were several major incidents (i.e., a stabbing, an inmate murdered by another inmate, the main walk-in refrigeration was broken into and emptied, etc.). All those incidents happened on my days off. I was told by several inmates that nothing serious happened on my watch, out of respect for me.

Don't get me wrong, the inmates always tried to "outfox" me. Sometimes I found them out, but often they succeeded (minor thefts, gambling, beer-making, etc.). Even though I enforced the rules, I treated them with dignity and did not misuse my authority.

Thus they respected me in turn and protected me and my reputation as an effective and efficient officer. On the other hand, an inmate's first priority is "self-preservation." So in truth, what they seemingly did for me, they really did for themselves. *They tried to "snow me" with respect so that I would perhaps become over confident and miss something. Let the games begin.*

The three years I spent at San Quentin enabled me to provide for my family while completing three years of graduate school. I received the master of divinity degree). Attending graduate school full-time while working forty to forty-eight hours a week, did not leave much time for family, studies, and sleep. I had to work a double shift (4:00 p.m. until 8:00 a.m.) once or twice a month and did not attend my classes on days following those sixteen-hour shifts. I also pastored a new church start every weekend. I was not conscious of the stress I was under during those three years. However, Linda said that occasionally, I would sit up in bed, in the middle of the night (still asleep) shouting some order to an inmate.

San Quentin provided me some very special experiences as well as contact with people of totally different lifestyles. Most of them did not have a personal relationship with God. When asked about life during those years of seminary and San Quentin, I told people that it was like living with one foot in heaven and one foot in hell. If they then asked, "Which foot was where?" (seminary vs. prison), I'd just smile, without giving an answer.

At that time, California had a terrible law that allowed an indeterminate sentence for many crimes. For example, there was one sentence for "one year to life." Then the prison system and parole board (not the courts) determined how long the inmate actually spent behind bars. I felt that was a very unfair sentence.

Linda also attended Golden Gate Seminary. Most of her time was consumed with her role of wife, mother, and homemaker. However, she made time to attend several classes each semester. She also babysat some children of working wives of students. She even took in ironing for some working wives.

She began attending classes at the beginning of my second year. However, Micah, our youngest son, was three months short of his second birthday and children had to be at least two years old to register for seminary preschool. Linda's first class of the day, began thirty minutes before my last class ended, so we had a thirty minute baby sitter problem.

Dr. Derwood Deere, my Old Testament professor, got wind of our need and he did not have a class that hour. Dr. Deere and a few students volunteered to take turns caring for Micah in the Student Center, two days a week for three months, until I got out of my class. When Micah turned two, we no longer had a problem.

Graduation from Seminary
and Move to Esparto

*D*uring my three years as a full-time graduate student at Golden Gate Seminary and three years full-time work at San Quentin, Linda and I were also able to help start a new church in Esparto, Yolo County, California, located about ninety miles from the seminary.

After completing my studies, we moved to Esparto and rented a house, with an option to purchase. Prior to that, we had been paid $5 a week; after moving to Esparto, we were paid $25 a week. I couldn't support my family on that small amount, so I transferred from San Quentin to the Correctional Facility at Vacaville, about thirty miles from Esparto.

The move to Esparto was good. I enjoyed being the pastor of Esparto Baptist Mission. We did not have a church building, but rented space in the VFW Hall. Actually, the VFW was in financial straits and needed us as much as we needed their building. A few years later, when their finances improved, they informed us that the building could no longer be used for a church. We had to move out. In time, God provided a permanent building for the church.

During our stay in Esparto, my brother Wayne and Naomi visited us. They attended morning worship with us, and Linda cooked chicken and rice casserole for lunch. Immediately after eating, Wayne and Nee left for the long drive home to El Segundo. A couple of hours before getting home, Wayne had an attack of appendicitis and had to stop for emergency surgery. Today, fifty years later, Wayne still won't eat chicken and rice casserole.

I did not enjoying working at the prison in Vacaville. Even though I had three years of experience, at a much more difficult prison, Vacaville treated me as a new hire and put me in a watch tower for many months. For me, that was like being in prison myself; plus, I struggled to stay alert and awake.

Vacaville would not give me an assignment with Sunday off, so I worked the first watch (midnight until 8:00 a.m.) in order to lead the Sunday morning and evening worship services in Esparto. I have a difficult time sleeping days, except for a short nap. Even when I was able to sleep, someone would often have a need that I needed to get up and address.

I worked every Sunday (midnight Saturday until 8:00 a.m. Sunday), drove home, bathed, dressed, and ate. Linda and I would then rush over to the VFW Hall to work with another member cleaning and airing it out (to get rid of the smell of beer from Saturday night). We also set up moveable plywood walls to divide the space into several Sunday school rooms.

Sometimes, I would get a good nap before evening worship. After evening worship and a quick meal, I was on the road again to be at the prison before midnight. After a year of that schedule, I was very weary, and my hair began to turn gray.

Moved from Esparto to Folsom, California

Eventually, First Baptist Church of Folsom, California, asked me to resign my position with the Department of Corrections and become their full-time pastor. I felt the move was God's will for me. *Although I left the small congregation in Esparto with regrets, I also felt that God had rescued me from unending weariness.*

Folsom is a suburb of Sacramento, the capital of California. It is also a prison town. I did not work at Folsom Prison but did some volunteer work with the inmates. Folsom is located in the vicinity of Coloma, where gold was discovered at Sutter's Mill and the ensuing nineteenth-century California Gold Rush. The American River flows out of nearby Folsom Lake and through Folsom.

Folsom, like all other places, had its own challenges, but we spent three very happy and fruitful years there. Many came to faith there. We still have several dear friends, including Lavelle and Ethelyn Prine, from those days. The people at Folsom loved us and accepted me as their pastor. Several even accepted me as a peer—that was a very special gift. Our children had many good friends. *It was the happiest time of our lives, until then.*

Missionary Call and Move from Folsom

We had no plans, or even thoughts, of becoming international missionaries. Little did we expect that the LORD would call us to leave Folsom and go to Indonesia. God's call was definite, but it came through a process.

In August 1968, during a Monday pastors' luncheon in Sacramento, I learned that the majority of requests for new personnel from the mission field were for people with my gifts and pastoral experience. That information came from Paul Box, IMB representative visiting Sacramento Baptist Association.

Earlier, I had subscribed to a children's magazine for our daughter Pam. Each month, a different country was highlighted. In early September, the first copy reached us. It was about Indonesia.

Also in September, I finally read Jess Fletcher's biography of Bill Wallace. That book had been in my personal library for about three years. Dr. Wallace had been a medical missionary to China. He was imprisoned after the Communist takeover of China. He died in prison, at the hand of his captors, a martyr for Christ.

The last Sunday in September 1968, I preached a sermon totally devoted to missions. I called it "Missions: God's Heartbeat." Until then, I had only included missions info and promotion in some of my sermons. Our church was scheduled to participate in a mission's conference in October and would have several missionary speakers in our church. My sermon was intended to increase interest in and support for missions, preparing for that conference.

During the sermon, I shared a testimony from the Philippines. A Filipino lady had just given her heart to Jesus. Suddenly, she began weeping loudly, not from joy, but from a deep grief. She also kept repeating something as she cried. At first, the missionary could not understand what she was saying because she was weeping so loudly. Finally, he heard her ask, "Why didn't you come last year?"

"I'm sorry," he said, "I came as quickly as I could." Then the lady expressed her grief, "My husband died last year. If he had heard the message of Jesus, he would have also believed."

The lady's words pierced my heart. I stopped preaching and began to weep myself. Thus God broke in on the preacher. I did not feel God calling me at that time. I didn't know what was happening. After a short while, I got myself under control and told the congregation, "I don't understand what is happening, but if God wants me to be a missionary, I will go." The pastor was converted during his own sermon.

Linda was sitting behind me in the choir. This was shocking news to her, although as a young girl, she thought God was calling her to missions. Later, after we married, she assumed that God wanted her to be a pastor's wife, not a missionary.

One day, that October, while reading the missionary prayer calendar, I came across the name of missionary, Everly Hayes. Everly was a nurse, who had worked with Dr. Bill Wallace, in China. One day, as she visited Dr. Wallace in the communist prison, he told her, "If the LORD allows me to get out of this prison, I would like to serve in Indonesia."

Dr. Wallace did not leave the prison alive; however, the prayer calendar indicated that Nurse Everly Hayes was serving in Indonesia. *(Note: In 1978, during our second furlough in California, Linda and I spoke in Davis, California, and stayed in the home of a Chinese American couple. The wife was a nurse. As a young nurse in China, she worked in Stout Memorial Hospital, under Dr. Bill Wallace. She said she and the other young nurses called Dr. Wallace "Papa.")*

We also saw two TV travel programs about Indonesia in September and October. Thus, five times within two months, Indonesia was thrust upon our mind.

At the big evening rally, during the mission conference, I heard several missionaries speak. One couple, Ralph and Lizette Bethea, were serving as medical missionaries in India. They had previously served in Indonesia. *God seemed to be speaking directly to my heart, and I was both emotional and acutely aware that He was calling me to go to Indonesia. I responded, "Okay, LORD, I will go."*

We wrote the International Mission Board, SBC and began the process of seeking missionary appointment to Indonesia. My qualifications were acceptable, but Linda needed twenty more college credits to qualify. Therefore, she enrolled in and completed eighteen semester hours at American River Community College that spring semester. IMB accepted her on promise of doing more college study when back in the USA for furlough which she fulfilled.

In May 1969, Linda and I flew to Dallas, Texas, where we were appointed at First Baptist Church and the SMU Fieldhouse, then returned to Folsom and continued to pastor until August.

In August, we sold some of our belongings, packed the rest for Indonesia. We moved from Folsom to Georgia to attend four months of intensive missionary orientation, at Calloway Gardens, in Pine Mountain, Georgia. We left for Georgia, stopping in Southern California, to visit my parents and give our dog, "Tippy" to them. We continued on to Galveston, to visit Mom and Dad Rountree, before finally reaching Georgia.

Missionary Orientation and Prep for Indonesia

Fall at Calloway Gardens was fantastic—flowers, trees, leaves, lakes, golf courses, and lots of new friends, who were also headed overseas. Three other couples (John and Sharon Gayle, Ken and Judy Milam, and Barry and Judy Nelson) were also bound for Indonesia. I had known the Gayles for several years; we attended Howard Payne and Golden Gate together. John and I worked at San Quentin together.

An added value for me. My Uncle Donald (Dad's brother), Aunt Bea and family lived in Columbus, Georgia, a half hour from Calloway Gardens. We spent several weekends with them. Uncle Donald and Aunt Bea had flown to Dallas for our missionary commissioning the previous May. In addition, Georgia is close to my roots in Florida. We were able to visit my maternal grandparents, Hugh Bishop and Gladys Wilson, as well as several cousins, in Gainesville, Florida.

Our visit with my Granddad Bishop would be my last; he passed away in 1973, a few weeks before we returned to the USA for our first furlough.

We experienced a death at orientation. Scott Rippato died of lymphoma. Judy and their children left orientation, not for a foreign field, but to stay in the USA.

In early December 1969, we finished our training and headed back to California for a January departure by ship. We drove via Jay, Florida, to visit my Granddad Beck. I helped him paint the trim on his house. Then on to Galveston, Texas, for another visit with Mom and Dad Rountree.

We were shocked to find Dad Rountree in the hospital. He had experienced another mild heart attack and needed to have his carotid artery replaced. He had the carotid artery on the other side replaced several years earlier. The doctors wanted to wait for him to regain strength from his heart attack before doing the surgery.

We enjoyed having two weeks with them, but left for California shortly before New Year. Fortunately, we took the southern route (I-10) to California, because there were terrible snow storms in Arizona, along I-40. We made it fine, with only light snowfall. However, two of our fellow missionaries, Rev. and Mrs. Howard Scott, who were scheduled to sail with us, traveled the northern route (I-40). The snow and ice were much worse on that route; their VW "Bug" skidded into an eighteen wheeler, and they were both killed. I attended Howard Payne with their daughter, Beth. At least three others from our orientation group died overseas, of illness, during their first term of service.

At Mom and Dad Beck's in Redondo Beach, California, we received a telephone call, on Tuesday, January 6, at 5:00 a.m., from the IMB (three time zones ahead of us, in Richmond, Virginia), informing us that our visa to Indonesia had not yet been granted, so we would not be able to depart on the 11 of January, as scheduled. Thus, we would not be able to go by ship; we would fly instead. That was a big disappointment.

The next morning (still very early), another call from the IMB. This time, the news was much better. Our visa had been granted; however, they would not be able to get our passports to us before we were to sail. However, we could sail to Honolulu without passports and were assured that our passports, with visas, would be in Hawaii, when we arrived. We did not mind that early call.

Grief and Hardships

*T*he *following day, Thursday, January 8, 1970, we got a call from Mom Rountree. Dad Rountree had gotten worse* and they could not delay his surgery any longer, because he was in danger of having a stroke. *Dad made it through surgery, but had a heart attack in the recovery room and passed away.*

Linda and I were able to get two tickets to return to Galveston. We left our children in California with my parents. I cannot remember if we flew Thursday afternoon or Friday morning. We all made it through the funeral on Saturday, but Mom Rountree was not feeling well on Saturday night.

We had to take an early Sunday morning limo to Houston, since we had a morning flight to Los Angeles. Our ship would sail that very afternoon. Mom Rountree seemed to be much better, but didn't get out of bed. She cried because we were leaving. She said she would never see us again. We assured her that she would be able to visit us in Indonesia. We hugged and kissed and said our good-byes. Fortunately, Aunt Billie, Dad Rountree's older sister from Florida, was going to stay with Mom for another week.

Things were hectic after we arrived back at my parent's home. We had to finish our income tax return. We had to sign the wills that Naomi, my sister-in-law, had prepared for us. There were several other smaller issues, but time was the enemy. Getting to the ship was a drama that I'll omit. I will only say my brother Wayne missed the presailing festivities because he made a speedy trip back to get our ship tickets. We arrived at the port with air tickets from Hong Kong to Jakarta with us, but our ship tickets to Hong Kong had fallen out of our travel envelope, at Mom and Dad's house.

The seas are rough in January. I am subject to seasickness, so had purchased seasick medication. However, those tablets made me drowsy, so although I did not get seasick, I did not feel good.

On Monday morning, Mom Rountree went to the doctor for a physical exam. She was given a clean bill of health. But sometime late that night, she suffered a stroke. She did not get up on Tuesday, and Aunt Billie found her and called an ambulance. Mom Rountree died on Wednesday, seven days after Dad Rountree's death.

We were in the middle of the Pacific when we received the radiogram about Mom Rountree's death. Her funeral was scheduled for Saturday morning, one week after Dad Rountree's funeral. We were devastated and had a difficult time thinking clearly. However, reality finally set in: we were in the middle of the ocean; we would not reach Honolulu until Friday afternoon. We would not be able to get home in time for the funeral; besides, we had very little cash and no credit card. My mom had our checkbook because she would manage our financial affairs while we were abroad.

Thus, we had to compose a reply expressing our grief and our help-lessness, stating that the funeral must go on without us. That was so difficult for us. Thankfully, there were several missionary friends from orientation sailing with us, and they wrapped themselves around our broken hearts. God is so good. *We were helpless, but God was not. As always "His grace is sufficient for us."*

Not being able to go home for Mom Rountree's funeral was not only difficult for us, it was difficult for Linda's only sister, Jerry (Geraldine), sixteen years Linda's senior. It was also difficult for Mom Rountree's siblings to understand "why we could not be there for the funeral of Linda's own mom."

As best we could, we followed the advice of Dr. Baker James Cauthen, president of the IMB. During the ceremony on the last day of orientation, he said, "Take your possessions in your hands, not in your hearts." But we had not prepared ourselves for the loss of our parents so soon.

Many years later, the case was somewhat similar in the deaths of my parents. I flew to California alone, in January 1983, for my mom's funeral. Our three oldest children, Pam, Steve, and Micah, were in Hardin Simmons University, Abilene, Texas. Linda and Matt, our youngest son, stayed in Tegal while I was gone.

Just getting to the USA was a major series of miracles. God enabled us to get a new clutch cable installed along the way while traveling four hours to two different cities to work through all the Indonesian government red tape to get a permit to leave and return to Indonesia, a testimony of God's sovereignty. Another miracle was that Linda drove our vehicle home the next day, without incident; yet the following day while driving in our town, both tie rods fell off of our front wheel assemblies. Had that happened on her trip home from Semarang, the previous day, she would have experienced a major accident.

I was able to stay with Dad in California for a month, except for the week I took off to visit the kids in Texas. Mom had been the family banker; she managed the finances. I was able to help Dad take care of necessary business and begin to heal, although he suffered from depression for several years after Mom's death from leukemia.

Dad's depression got so bad that I prayed about resigning and going home to watch over him. But then God solved the problem. Dad fell in love with June Ruiz, the mother of Connie, one of our daughters-in-love. They were married, but we could not attend.

In January 1993, ten years after my Mom's death, Dad had a massive heart attack. He dropped dead early one morning as he got up.

Linda, Matt, and I were in New Delhi, India, when we received news of Dad's sudden death. However, we could not get out of India because the airlines and airport workers were all on strike. The government had attempted to circumvent the strike by hiring Kazakhstani planes and crews to keep people in the air. However, the day before Dad passed away, a Kazakh plane crashed upside down on the runway, and the Indian government closed the airport.

Thus, we were trapped in New Delhi. So, I had to make the difficult telephone call home saying that we could not come home. That was not only difficult on us, it was difficult on my siblings and on June, Dad's wife of six years.

My grief over Dad's death seemed to be aggravated by not being able to return home to share our grief with the family. A supposed situation arose after Dad's death, and I made phone calls back to each of my siblings. *I did not handle the situation very well, and that resulted in additional stress for each of my siblings.* Nevertheless, even as they had forgiven me for the sins of my childhood, they have also forgiven me of my many faults during adulthood. That is grace; not based on my merit, but on their love. I am grateful.

I add two thoughts along this line: Satan is called the accuser, and that he is. He defeats many by reminding us of our sins and shortcomings and casting doubt on our forgiveness, because we are unworthy. He is correct that we are unworthy, but God's grace is based on His character, not ours, and His grace is sufficient to forgive, renew, and make us useful to Him and others.

I have also experienced Satan as the great "excuser." He enabled me to excuse my childhood sins. Thus I was able to seemingly forget them completely, and I "seemed" unscathed by them for many years. Later, I learned it was not that easy for those I sinned against. In truth, it was not that easy for me either, because *those sins, although successfully forgotten in my conscious mind, dominated my subconscious mind and held me in bondage and made me vulnerable to Satan's constant accusations* of being unfit for God's grace.

I am grateful that God's loving grace brought those terrible sins back into my conscious memory and led me into repentance. I also confessed my sins to my siblings. Not only did God forgive me, He also worked in the hearts of my siblings to forgive an undeserving older brother.

While on the subject of difficulties, *another stressful time for missionaries and missionary kids is when our kids begin going away to boarding school during high school and especially when they return to the USA for college.*

Our children's departure not only brings separation, it sometimes includes troubling situations for our children. Some of those situations necessitate missionary parents leaving the field to return to the USA to help their young adult children.

When Matt, our youngest, left Wachita Baptist University early, we wondered if we should return to the USA to provide support and a home base for him.

However, Sharon and Mike, my sister and brother-in-love, then living in Fairfield, California, opened their hearts and home to Matt, even as they had done for many other college kids. They have blessed many families. *What a blessing Sharon and Mike have been to us. That relationship also gave us Jodi White, a friend of Mike and Sharon's daughters, to become our third daughter-in-love.*

No matter the situation, God always keeps His promise, "My grace is sufficient for you." Praise the LORD, *He is constant. The only variable is "our faith" or "lack of faith" during hard times.*

Times like those are real hardships, but generally, people need not feel sorry for missionaries. I usually told concerned people, "Don't feel sorry for me. In truth, I feel sorry for you, because you don't get to enjoy the blessings, of people and experiences, we have."

Hong Kong by Sea, Followed by Flight to Jakarta

We sailed aboard the USS *President Cleveland*, an American president liner. Their ships carried both passengers and cargo.

Actually, January is not the best month for crossing the Pacific Ocean, because the seas are very rough in January.

The crossing by ship was a good thing for us. It gave us rest from the preparations for leaving the USA. We also received loving support from over twenty missionaries who sailed with us. God used our three weeks aboard the USS *President Cleveland* to begin the healing process of our grief from the deaths of Linda's parents.

The voyage from Long Beach, California, to Hong Kong included four intermediary stops: Honolulu; Yokohama, Japan; Kobe, Japan; and Taipei, Taiwan. Thus we were able to ease into Asia before actually arriving in Indonesia.

The passage was pleasant, and our kids had a ball. In the beginning, our "lower first class" cabins were just above the waterline, the kids were in another room, and the baths were down the hall. But we were all content, except that I was taking seasick pills that I purchased before sailing, and they kept me drowsy. I felt like a "zombie" most of the time, but I didn't get seasick even though the seas were rough.

Things became better after we arrived in Honolulu. We enjoyed touring around the city by foot. When we walked around on land, we had the sensation that we were still aboard ship and the land seemed to rock. That helped because when we boarded the ship to depart Honolulu, we seemed to have gained our "sea legs" and the rocking of the ship no longer bothered us. I also learned the crew gave out seasick pills that didn't make you drowsy, so I took them, and I felt good for the rest of the voyage, even though we had very rough seas as we skirted a typhoon.

The biggest improvement came in our cabins. A large number of "first class" passengers left the ship in Honolulu. The ship's purser was very gracious and upgraded all the missionaries to true "first class." Our cabins were not the luxury staterooms of "upper first class." But even though our new cabin assignments were not large or luxurious, they were nice, and each cabin had a window and its own bathroom. *They were much nicer than we deserved.*

Attitude is very important. I personally reject the concept that I deserve special treatment because I am a minister. God's calling gives no special entitlements. On the other hand, His grace always far surpasses what we deserve.

The ship's crew was very accommodating, especially to children. There was an event coordinator just for the kids. Our kids were kept busy and happy. However, the best thing for our kids was the presence of many missionary kids, whom they had come to know during missionary orientation in Georgia.

Children were required to eat at the early sitting for meals; of course, our fellow missionaries chose to eat then too, in order to be with their children. However, because we didn't have our tickets with us when we first boarded, Linda and I were not able to sign up for our meal seats until after the ship sailed. By the time we signed up for meal seating, the early sitting was full. We had to take the second sitting, the one for adults only. We were a bit upset because we couldn't be with our children or our friends.

The ship's purser assured us that our kids would be fine without us, but that we would be able to switch to the first sitting when we arrived in Honolulu. Well, our kids had a ball, at a table of all kids. Joe, their African American waiter, was excellent. He knew how to make the kids happy, and all the kids at Joe's table loved him.

Micah wanted to help Joe set the table, etc. But Joe said he was sorry, but Micah would not be able to help because waiters had to dress formally. The next meal, Micah showed up thirty minutes before the meal. He was dressed in black dress slacks, a red blazer, a white shirt, and a black bow tie. What could Joe do? Micah helped Joe every meal after that. Micah, aged seven, was "big stuff."

Linda and I enjoyed the late sitting. Our table mates were wealthy older people, several of whom were widows. They were all very sweet, but none of them seemed to have any purpose in life. They seemed to just exist, enjoying their riches, but really just waiting for death. None of them acknowledged a relationship with God.

One widow at our table thought it was so romantic that Mom Rountree died a week after Dad Rountree's death. She said she would have preferred that in her case; her husband had been dead for several years. She asked us what kind of food we would miss the most. We said, "Mexican food." We told her that we had attempted to order canned corn tortillas, to send to Indonesia, but the store did not follow through with our order. A few months later, we received a package of several cans of corn tortillas from that lady; another example how God has blessed us even through unbelievers.

While aboard the ship, we crossed time zones nearly nightly. That gave us an extra hour to sleep most nights. We didn't actually sleep more but stayed up an extra hour nearly nightly without paying for it the next morning. We also enjoyed port calls in Honolulu; Yokahama, Japan, Kobe, Japan; as well as Taipei, Taiwan. Finally, after nearly three, mostly enjoyable, weeks at sea, the five Milams and the five Becks left the ship in Hong Kong. The *President Cleveland* sailed on to Manila, the Philippines, without us.

After three days of shopping and sightseeing in Hong Kong, we arrived at the Hong Kong airport and were informed that the time of departure for our flight to Jakarta, Indonesia, had been revised and that our flight had departed three hours earlier. We were, however, able to reschedule and depart several hours later. After receiving our new schedules, Ken Milam sent a telegram to Jakarta to inform our office of our new arrival time, flight number, etc.

Indonesia at Last

We arrived in Jakarta around midnight, near the end of January 1970. It was sweltering hot and very humid. Air-conditioning was several years in the future. There were thousands of insects, most varieties of which were unknown to any of us. We were sweaty and very weary. Cheri Milam and our Pam were somewhat terrified by all the large insects. Probably the Beck and Milam boys were as well, but they tried to appear brave.

Immigration and Custom lines seem to take forever, but finally, we got through with all our passports stamped and our luggage in tow. Next surprise, no one was there to meet us. Our telegram finally arrived two weeks after we did. Ken Milam had the foresight to bring a telephone number with him; phonebooks were nonexistent. Yes, they had been there to meet us earlier, but no, they would not be able to return to get us now. Leon Mitchell did talk to the taxi drivers by phone, and cab prices were agreed upon. The Milams left in one direction for the mission guesthouse. The Becks left in another direction, for the home of missionaries, Bill and Chris Hailey and sons, old friends from Galveston. Since it was so late, well after 2:00 a.m., we didn't sit up talking very long.

Beginning around 5:00 a.m., we were awakened by strange sounds on the street. First, we heard a musical sound of wood striking wood and then a voice calling out "Bakso! Bakso!" Bakso is a type of soup eaten for breakfast or any other meal during the day. A little later, a voice called out, "Sapu ... sapu." Later we learned that was a broom salesman. Sapu is the Indonesian word for broom. The new strange noises, voices, and smells continued in the darkness of early *morning, like an unseen pageant parading through our ears, nostrils, and imaginations.*

Morning begins early in Indonesia, so that was the end of our short night's sleep. Just as well because after breakfast, Bill and Chris loaded us in their Volkswagen bus for the drive to our new home city. The trip to Bandung, normally a four-hour drive, took about seven hours due to stops along the way—to taste new fruits and delicacies, enjoy mountain views with tea plantations, terraced rice fields, etc., and to eat a meal in Bogor with the Trotter family.

Language Study, Bandung, Indonesia

B andung had a population of a million people. It was appropriately called the Garden City of Indonesia. A beautiful old city with a very mild temperature. Mild temperature is a blessing in a hot humid tropical world. We were surprised to discover that we would be living in a plain, but fairly nice two-story house instead of a "grass hut."

Actually, there were three other missionary houses close to ours. It was not a compound because there were no high walls and each house had its own driveway to the street. Two houses faced one street. The other two were behind ours and faced another street. Our street was named JL Kapt. Tendian, in honor of an army officer murdered during the attempted Communist coup d'état, a little more than three years earlier, on September 30, 1966.

A couple of blocks down the hill from us, a house had been rented for the Milam family. We were in missionary orientation with them and traveled to Indonesia with them. Their three children, a girl and two boys, were almost identical ages with ours. There were also countless Indonesian kids living nearby.

Our year of language study was comfortable and pleasant, with new friends and wonderful excursions into our new country. We built an A-frame bamboo playhouse on stilts, in the backyard, to accompany an existing swing set. We hiked in low mountains; climbed down into extinct volcanoes (which erupted again, a few years later); adapted to exotic foods, fruits, and cultures; made many new friends and even learned to speak Bahasa Indonesia. I also endured eleven months of the "Bandung trots," which enabled me to lose the twenty-two pounds I had gained aboard ship.

After several months in Bandung, I began borrowing English language "Bible story films" from our Baptist *penerbitan* (publication office). We hung a bedsheet up on our empty carport, and neighbors filled our driveway and front yard to view the films shown each week. I enlisted a Sundanese Christian to give a running commentary on the film, in the Sunda language.

The final six months of language study, I served as interim pastor for the English language worship services of Indonesian language "Gereja Baptis Wastukencana" of Bandung.

First Work Assignment, Tegal, Central Java

After a year of language study and two more months acquiring a house to rent, we moved from West Java to the city of Tegal, in Central Java, in April 1971. We continued to enjoy the beauty of rice fields and could see mountains, but we lived in the flatlands.

Our new city was on the north coast of Java, facing the Java Sea. Gone was the mild temperature of Bandung, instead were hot humid coastal plains filled with mosquitoes, odors of drying fish, and the sound of the call to worship from mosques. Unlike Bandung, Tegal was not a pretty city. It had a population of one hundred thousand squeezed into a mere one square mile.

We could not get to the beach in most places, because the coast was nearly filled with fishing villages. However, the beach was accessible in Tegal. We only waded in the beach, instead of swimming because the beach was polluted and often muddy from several contaminated streams and rivers emptying into the sea. However, it was good for picnics, and later it was a good place to teach our children to drive—the Vespa first and later the VW bus.

About two months after moving to Tegal, Linda experienced excruciating pain in her lower abdomen. We had not yet made the acquaintance of any physicians. I asked several new friends and was given the name of Dr. Oui, a Chinese Indonesian, who spoke good English. That was important because we had not yet learned Indonesian words for medical problems.

Dr. Oui thought Linda might have an atopic (tubular) pregnancy. She would need emergency surgery; however, he advised us not to go to the hospital in Tegal. The hospital was not sanitary and did not even have any semimodern equipment. Dr. Oui referred us to the Catholic Hospital in Semarang, a hard three-hour drive.

We made the trip, and Dr. Oui's diagnosis was correct. Linda had successful surgery to remove the affected ovary and tube. The doctor told us that Linda's fallopian tube had probably ruptured before we reached the hospital, but by some miracle, she did not bleed to death. I told the doctor that God put His finger on the tube and stopped the bleeding. Avery and Shirley Willis, fellow missionaries, kept our children for two weeks while Linda healed. God was very good to us because that crisis was life threatening.

We worked hard seeking to reach people in the city of Tegal and in the countryside, as far as two hours away. Progress was slow. The common people were somewhat open; some were very responsive. However, small numbers of radical Muslims were able to control the unsophisticated masses. The radical Muslims were radical in religion; they were not terrorists, although they used strong intimidation on the masses.

That first assignment was good but was the most difficult we experienced in our thirty-three years overseas. Letters of support from family never ceased, but after a couple of years, letters from friends, busy with their own lives, slowly ceased. *One day, while feeling sorry for myself, I said aloud, "Lord, I could die over here and no one would know it." I heard no reply with my ears, but my heart heard God say, "I would know."*

During the summer of 1971, two seminary students, Bambang Subagio and Sutoyo Louis Sigar, stayed in our home for nearly three months. They made many contacts for us, some of which would later come to the Lord. They also helped me understand and maneuver many cultural experiences that I had not learned during language study.

In the fall of 1972, we started a new congregation in Tegal by merging three small home Bible study groups. All the members, except Linda,

Pam, and I and Pak and Ny (Mr. and Mrs.) *Soeyatno, a young Javanese couple, were new believers—including our sons, Steve and Micah. We rented the public swimming pool one Sunday morning, during a vacant hour, and baptized the new believers.*

That Sunday evening, we met for worship in a small building behind our house. That evening, we organized ourselves as Gereja Baptis Kalvari (Calvary Baptist Church) *and celebrated the Lord's Supper together. Pak Soeyatno (Yatno) had come to faith several years earlier, in his hometown of Jogakarta, prior to moving to Tegal to work as a low-level bank employee. His wife had also become a believer there.*

Pak Yatno had suggested the name for the new congregation. Since he had church experience, I asked him to prepare the Lord's Supper, and he agreed. When we entered the building that evening, I realized that I should have helped in the preparations for the Lord's Supper. Pak Yatno had purchased a strong medicinal wine given to pregnant ladies, and the smell was overpowering. We made it through the evening, though I'll say the wine burned all the way down. The next time, I suggested we use Fanta Grape; we were thereafter thankful for the Coca-Cola company.

Pak Yatno became a dear friend and a very teachable lay leader for the congregation. I learned to stay low key and from time to time would make a gentle suggestion and never mention it again. After a few weeks or months, he would sometimes propose some of those suggestions back to me, as if they had originated with him. In a way, they did; he let them percolate in his mind, praying about it, and it then was his idea. I would simply say, "Yes, that might work. Should we try it?" I have learned that we can get more done if we don't care who gets the credit. I also learned to be happy that Yatno didn't accept all my suggestions; some were not appropriate.

The place of worship was moved to the Soeyatno's rented home in August 1973, when we left for a six-month furlough in California. The following year, the congregation purchased a small plot of land; however, the local government never gave permission to build a place of Christian worship.

Several years later, they sold their land and used that money to purchase a small house and convert it into a house of worship. Many scattered small groups of new believers (house churches) were planted in the countryside. We were also able to help rejuvenate an existing church in the city of Pekalongan, an hour east of Tegal.

Three representative vignettes of new believers in Tegal:

1. Mrs. Supadmo, a tall stately elderly Javanese lady, lived on the edge of Tegal. Her husband's second wife lived with them. I met Mrs. Supadmo through her grandson, Suproptono (Tono), who lived with his grandparents in order to attend a technical high school, in Tegal. Tono had been led to Christ by the two seminary students, who stayed with us. Mrs. Supadmo could not read Indonesian or Javanese, but one day she told me that she could read the old Javanese script. Written Javanese had been changed to the Latin alphabrt some fifty years earlier. It took a while, but I finally found someone in a distant village, who still had an old Bible in the Javanese script. He said he would trade it for a Bible in English. A few weeks later, I returned to his village and gave him one of my personal English Bibles. I will never forget the smile on Mrs. Supadmo's face when I placed the Javanese Bible in her hands. She opened it and began reading aloud from the first chapter of Genesis. Tears of joy streamed down her cheeks as she read God's word for the first time in her life. A few months later Mrs. Supadmo gave her heart to Jesus. Over the years, many came to Christ, but getting that Bible to that dear lady was one of the best things I ever did.

2. Mr. and Mrs. Mul and their eighteen year old daughter, each came to the Lord, after Mr. Mul's retirement from the Army. His pension was very minimal. A couple of years later, the quiet dumpy Mr. Mul told me about a neighbor, who continually asked him, "How much money do they give you

to attend that Baptist church?" A bewildered Mul would always tell him, "They don't give me anything, instead, I give money to my church." His neighbor did not believe Mul and one day finally said, "Mul, I have watched you since you started going to church. I noticed you painted your house, you purchased a TV, and some other nice things. I know your pension has not increased, so you must be getting extra money from somewhere." Mr. Mul laughed and chided his neighbor, "If you have been watching me, why didn't you notice that God has changed my life. I quit smoking and selfishly wasting money like I used to do. That is a blessing from God; so now without any increase in my pension, I can do things for my family that I could not do before I received Jesus. So that is how I was able to paint my house, buy a TV and some other nice things for my wife and daughter."

3. A man on a mission: Many people visited our home; some were friends, while some were people I didn't know. When guests visit you in Indonesia, you invite them in, serve them hot tea and biscuits (cookies/crackers) and chat. When a stranger comes, the culture required that you make small talk for at least fifteen minutes before you ask them, "Is there something important on your mind?" (polite speech for, "Why did you come?"). One day a tall slim man with long hair knocked on our door. He was about 35 years old. He told me his name was Tudjin, he was married and he and his wife had three young children. He politely asked if he could talk to me about something very important. I thought maybe he wanted help. I was surprised when he quickly got down to business. Someone had told him that he could learn about "Tuhan" (God) from me.

So, I began to share the "good news about God and His love for us," even before the tea and biscuits were served. After about an hour, Tudjin asked if he could return with his wife, on another day. When he returned with Mrs. Tudjin, I learned that he was a "becak" (pedicab) driver. They soon began attending Bible study and worship. It was not long before they placed their faith in Christ, received 'believer's baptism' and became faithful members of the Tegal congregation.

Tegal became our home for nine good years. I was busy trying to evangelize, conduct Bible studies, and start new churches. Linda homeschooled our children, maintained our home, and worked in church. We were the only Americans in Tegal, but there was a small international community, and we got together from time to time. There were two Dutch couples, one couple from Sri Lanka, and another from Bangladesh, none of whom were believers. Those families had a total of six children, all younger than ours.

Later, a British family of believers, David and Margo Thomson and their children, moved to Tegal during our first "home leave." We became good friends with them and enjoyed a Bible study together each Sunday. David taught our boys poetry, for Linda, who was homeschooling them. Later their work with the UN took them to the Philippines. *In the late 1990s, Linda and I were blessed to visit the Thomsons in their home in Lossiemouth, Scotland.*

Steve and Micah had many friends. They also had near complete freedom and an enjoyable childhood. Matt was born August 5, 1995, while we lived in Tegal. He was actually born at Baptist Hospital, Kediri, East Java.

Pam had a fair first year in Tegal. She played with neighbors and rode her bike around town with her brothers. However, being tall for her age and rapidly developing into a young lady, her early semifreedom was short-lived in a Muslim society.

Even worse, Indonesian girls her age tended to be immature and culturally parochial. So, Pam had no local friends who appreciated her as a person. Therefore, a lonely Pam tended to stay at home reading or playing the piano. Deliverance for her came a few years later when she was able to go to the international school in Jakarta. She boarded in a dormitory provided by our mission.

Even though Tegal was difficult to penetrate, I was contented and felt that was where God wanted us at that time. However, it was not easy to watch our daughter struggle and become unhappy. That was one of the many times that we had to walk by faith alone, because what I saw was difficult to understand and deal with.

The years in Tegal were not all bad for Pam. There were many good times as well: family picnics, swimming in mountain streams (often with other missionary families), and seasonal gatherings like mission meetings, missionary kid (MK) camps, etc. As I have already mentioned, Pam eventually moved to Jakarta to enter the ninth grade at Jakarta International School, which at least ended her loneliness. Later, Steve and finally Micah each moved to Jakarta for high school as well.

Picture of Beck family, at home in Tegal, Indonesia, 1978. Linda & Matthew sitting inside 'becak' (pedicap). Standing, L–R: Pamela, Micah & Fred. Seated on driver's seat, Stephen.

The only time I considered quitting and going home was when one of our kids in Jakarta faced a situation that I viewed to be potentially disastrous. We were at a prayer retreat when I learned about the situation. I was so alarmed that I immediately decided (without even praying), to go home pack our bags, drive to Jakarta, pick up our kids, and leave Indonesia.

I told our special speaker the situation and my quick decision. He asked a simple question, "Have you ever surrendered your child to God?"

"Yes!" I quickly replied.

"Then, this is God's problem, not yours," he said. "Do you think He is capable of dealing with it?"

We talked a long time, then prayed earnestly together. *I poured out my heart to God and entrusted this problem to Him.*

The prayer retreat ended the next morning, and we drove home. I went to the telephone office, called Jakarta, and learned the "would-be problem" was already solved. God is so awesome.

One common method I used to try to begin new work was to travel by Vespa scooter throughout our district meeting new people. Most of them claimed to be Muslim but were really animists (a primitive spirit religion), with a Muslim veneer. Men often invited me into their home to drink tea and chat with them.

Neighbors saw the foreigner come and would come to the house where I visited. Thus, I could meet several men at one time. Farmers were usually in their fields from 6:00 a.m. until about 10:00 a.m., then back in their fields after 3:00 p.m. They rested in the midday hours. That gave me a daytime window with farmers. Teachers, etc., were home in the later afternoon hours. During my initial visit, I shared my personal experience with the Lord and finally leave. If I was still given a warm reception, after hearing my testimony, I would return to that home in two or three weeks.

On subsequent visits, I would interject Bible verses into the conversation, as those verses related to the subjects of conversation or to answer their questions. After a few months, as the men began to trust me, I told them if at least three heads of household requested, I would teach them six or eight Bible studies about what Christians believe. I told them those studies had "no strings attached" (they had no obligations after that). If the group was really interested in what I taught, I later told them we could extend the studies if they so requested.

The "three heads of household" minimum was an arbitrary number that I set. My intent was that if they believed in the Lord, they would not be alone and could encourage one another in the faith. My goal was to introduce them to God's word then allow the Holy Spirit to move the word of God from their head to their heart, thus allow the Spirit of God to bring them into relationship with Jesus.

Tegal was a tough assignment, but we stayed there for nine years—our longest assignment in Indonesia. The people were somewhat open to the Gospel, but they were fearful of their radical Islamic leaders. Our Jakarta office made several requests for us to consider moving from Tegal to Klaten. I resisted those requests for a couple of years because I knew, if we moved, the mission would not replace us.

Finally, one event broke my resistance to a move. I had begun a home Bible study in a far-out village. It had grown rapidly, and after several weeks, about twenty-five local village men studied with me each week. The small home, with dirt floor, was packed, while women and children joined us by standing outdoors, at the door and open windows. It was the most successful home study I had begun up until then and I could hardly contain my joy.

Then one week, only six men attended, with no one standing outside. I was surprised but did not question the men, assuming there was a marriage, death, circumcision, or some other village event going on. The following week, only three men attended; something drastic was happening. The men revealed that strong opposition has arisen from radical Muslims of the area.

The villagers were told that the holiest mosque in Saudi Arabia had been invaded and occupied by armed Christians. The mosque had been invaded and occupied, but the perpetrators were radical Muslims, not Christians. Thus, an untruth was used to intimidate unsophisticated villagers who were studying with a Christian man. It was further stated that any married man, who becomes a Christian, must leave the village and leave his family behind. Furthermore, anyone becoming a Christian could not be buried in the area. If they died, their body would be left to rot above ground (at least they were not told they would be killed).

At that point, none of those men had become believers. Thus none of them had the indwelling Spirit of God to encourage, assure, and strengthen them. It seemed evident that my presence with them would continue to become a problem for them. So, I told them there was a small group of Pentecostal believers a mile farther down the path. Each week, I parked my vehicle near the highway and walked a mile to their village. If they wanted to continue to study, they could walk to the village where the Pentecostals met.

That evening, heavy rain began to fall as I walked the mile back to my vehicle. I had a big umbrella to shelter me from the rain, yet my clothes became wet anyway—not from the rain, but from my tears. I was brokenhearted because those men were so close to believing, but the "evil one" had used lies and intimidation to snatch the truth from them before it had penetrated their hearts. My enemy was Satan, not the radical Muslims.

I took that event as a possible sign, so I finally agreed to consider a move to Klaten. There were many needs and opportunities in Klaten, yet without the intense opposition I continually faced in Tegal. Ed Sanders, my supervisor, mentor and friend spent a week with me in the Klaten area. After that survey, I finally agreed to move. But I made a condition, that I would be allowed to drive back to Tegal one weekend each month (five-hour drive), for six months to further prepare the Tegal church's leadership.

Second Assignment 1980, Klaten, Central Java

*W*e enjoyed five good years in the Klaten area. We were even busier than before. We were involved in more church plants, maintained many house churches, and taught many training courses throughout the region.*

Some of my work in the Klaten area was to follow up on work started by Ed Sanders; work begun while he had lived an hour away, in Jogjakarta. Those churches and mission points had not had much attentions since Ed's move to Jakarta, to lead our mission.

Most of my new work was directed by the local leadership of the Gabungan (Baptist Convention). That in itself was good, but I felt like my work was more like that of a quasi director of missions, yet without the authority. It had been an area of rapid church growth; but growth had slowed, due in part to a lack of vision on the part of established pastors of that area.

Besides work, there were several recreational opportunities outside Klaten. The area had scattered spring-fed swimming pools (chilly water) with rock bottoms, where you could swim with the fish. We occasionally got together with other missionary families in a mountain cottage in Kaliurang, on the slopes of an active volcano, Gunung Merapi (Mountain of Fire), an hour northwest of Klatan.

While in Klaten, one by one, our three older children returned to the USA to enter Hardin Simmons University, Abilene, Texas. We were all blessed because, each of them met their mates there. Pam met

Mark Hotmann, of Amarillo, Texas. Steve met Connie Ruiz, of Tacoma, Washington, and Micah met Alison Hall, of Abilene, Texas.

We enjoyed a furlough with Crescent Heights Baptist Church, Abilene, Texas, in 1981. Our three older kids were students at Hardin Simmons University. Matt started first grade and Linda also studied at HSU. Prior to that, we and our children had furloughed near my parents, in Redondo Beach, California, in 1973 and again in 1978,

My mom died of leukemia, in January 1983. I flew to USA for her funeral, but high costs necessitated that Linda and Matt not go.

Pam and Mark settled in Amarillo, Mark's home town. While working at a temporary job, Pam met Nancy Mays, the chairperson of the FBC Missionary House Committee. The two of them signed us up to furlough there in mid-1985, prior to our move to Ambon.

Many years earlier, in the mid-1970s, we had received a general letter, to IMB missionaries, from FBC Amarillo with an invitation to furlough with them. After reading that letter, with picture and details about the house, I remarked to Linda, "Nice home, but who wants to live in Amarillo?" Never say never.

When we arrived in Amarillo, in June 1985, we met our first grandchild, Khara Elese Hotmann (named after my mother). Khara was born February 3, 1985; however, she died June 25th of the same year.

We rejoice that God enabled us to know and hold her, albeit in a hospital room. None of us were prepared to give her up. It is hard to lose a grandchild, but even more difficult to watch your children agonize over the loss of their child. We hold dear the opportunity to have been with Pam and Mark during their darkest days thus far. (Note: As I write this "Note," my manuscript is with the publisher and I am working with them about editing. Suddenly it dawned on me that if we had furloughed prior to moving to Ambon, instead of after, although we would have been with Khara when she died, we would have returned to Indonesia after her funeral, but we would not have been able to be with Mark and Pam during their (and our) difficult months following Khara's death. God knows everything and

He used the situation in Indonesia to place us in Amarillo at the best time for our family needs. Thank You LORD.

We were not able to furlough where Steve or Micah and their families lived. A furlough home has to be reserved well in advance; however, during those years, both those sons were more mobile, making it difficult to know where they would be living next and seemingly impossible to find a place on short notice.

During our second furlough in Amarillo (1988), we decided to eventually retire there. After that, we never considered any other place for furlough or retirement. Amarillo became our home. We enjoyed five six-month furloughs with FBC Amarillo prior to retirement. In all, we enjoyed eight six-month furloughs over our thirty-three and a half years overseas.

We were under a lot of stress during that second furlough in Amarillo. The Indonesian government was not renewing many mission- ary visas, and we had lost at least a third of our missionary force there. I kept questioning God, "Why are you allowing this, Lord, don't you know the work is going well, many people are being saved, many new churches are being planted?" I kept complaining to God, but He didn't seem to respond. I didn't want to consider that my attitude, not God, was the problem.

While still in turmoil over the loss of missionary colleagues in Indonesia. I was asked to speak to our church's Acteens (missions service and education organization for junior/senior high girls). They were on a retreat and stayed at the FBC cabin, at the local Baptist encampment. The day I spoke to the girls, an amazing thing hap- pened. *At the same time that I was speaking to the girls, God was dealing with me, in my heart.*

I am not aware of seeing any vision, yet without seeing with my eyes or hearing with my ears, something happened. It was as if I was climbing a tall mountain; it was cold, dark, and foggy. I could not see anything. However, the wind was blowing, and there seemed to be strong downdrafts. I felt as if I was about to slip and fall off a cliff; my emotions were raging.

I was complaining to God again, and I threw His Word back in His face. I quoted my life verse, Proverbs 3:5 and 6 to God. "Trust in the Lord with all your heart, And do not lean on your own understanding. In all your ways acknowledge Him, and He will make your paths straight."

I yelled at God, "I have done what you said, Lord! Why haven't you kept your end of the bargain?" Then it was as if God tapped me on the shoulder and said, "Turn around." In my mind's eye, I turned around and—wow … there was no more darkness; the sun was bright, all was calm, and the path behind me was not cliffs of a mountain, but rather a long flat straight highway stretching to the horizon from which I had come.

Then God spoke softly, "See, I have kept my end of the bargain, now turn around and continue to walk by faith." So I turned around, and I was seemingly immediately back on the dark dangerous mountain. However, I was no longer alone; the words of God, "Continue to walk by faith," were gently throbbing in my heart. God keeps His promises. He is in control, and I need not worry or doubt; just trust Him and continue to walk by faith. The stress was gone; peace and hope were renewed.

Linda says I cannot multitask, do two things at once; she is correct. But somehow that day, two things were going on simultaneously. I did communicate with those girls, at the encampment, even while God was teaching me something about "mountain climbing." *The funny thing is, I don't remember what I taught the girls that day, but I do remember what the Lord taught me about mountain climbing.*

Third Assignment: Ambon, Maluku, Indonesia

After a request from the Indonesian Baptist Convention, we moved to Ambon in January 1985, prior to our third furlough, our first in Amarillo. We wanted to get settled and complete all the government red tape so we could hit the ground running after furlough. Ambon, the capital of the Molucca Islands (one thousand island province of Muluku), is a beautiful horseshoe-shaped island. The ocean is deep and beautiful. The deepwater harbor comes right up to the edge of downtown Ambon. The harbor inside the horseshoe is five hundred feet deep. There was a car ferry that crosses the harbor, shortening the long drive around the bend to the airport.

The majority people of Muluku are good musicians with beautiful voices. That is partly due to their traditional Christian heritage (begin singing in church at early age). A number of Indonesia's pop singers, as well as many of the top religious singers, hail from Muluku. Some of their music sounds Hawaiian. The minority people are Muslims. Some of those are native to Muluku, but most were resettled from Java by the Indonesian government.

Our favorite beach was Natsepa. It is in a protected cove with almost no waves. The water is crystal clear and the bottom is white sand. Our church hired vehicles to go there for baptisms. Everyone took food to share, and it was a great church picnic. Linda, Matt, and I went there nearly every week to swim and to eat *rujak* (a yummy local fruit salad topped with a brown sugar and chili pepper sauce).

Ambon "Manise" (Sweet Ambon) was Linda's favorite Indonesian assignment. It was there that she blossomed the most and was the most fruitful up to that time. Most fruitful, partially because she no longer homeschooled, partially because of the openness of the Ambonese people, but mostly by God's grace.

Linda home schooled Matt, as she had done for our older three children. However, while in Ambon, *Matt's educational needs necessitated his going to Surabaya (on Java) to board with Charles and Barbara Cole, fellow missionaries. He went there to attend Surabaya International School, for second semester of seventh and entire eighth grade. SIS only went through eighth grade. The Coles, already dear friends, were God's blessing for us.*

For his ninth grade, Matt moved to the Christian Missionary Alliance School, Sentani, Irian Jaya (Indonesian New Guinea). It was three hours, by jet plane, from Ambon. A teacher family boarded Matt and another boy in their home. God is so good.

My work schedule was two weeks in Ambon, followed by one week on the much larger Island of Seram. On travels to Seram, I carried a large backpack filled with clothes, sleeping gear, and books (lending library). I rode my Vespa to a people ferry, about a half hour from our rented house, on the outskirts of our city.

Upon reaching the ferry harbor, I paid laborers to help me load the Vespa onto the roof of the ferry. Then I settled in for a four-hour crossing. The sea was deep, the waves were often rough, but we were always within sight of land. When the sea was calm, dolphins and/ or flying fish entertained us along the way. I remembered Rudyard Kipling's poems, **"On the Road to Mandalay"** … "where the flyin'-fishes play" and **"Gunga Din"** … "you're a better man than I, Gunga Din," two high school favorites. Perhaps it was God's hint about future places of service in India and Burma.

Rain or shine, I sat on the top deck in front of the pilot. I could always see land in the distance; that was my remedy against seasickness. When the moon was full, the sailing was smooth (except in January and February). Less than full moon meant rough seas. As I write this many years later, every time I see a full moon, I smile and say to myself, "The sea is smooth in Ambon tonight."

At Seram's harbor, a few miles from Masohi, the Vespa was offloaded, and away I went. I stopped in Masohi to report in with the police and to let the family of Pak Stev, a federal judge and a deacon in the Masohi fellowship, know I had arrived and was going on to Waipia.

The trip to Waipia began by Vespa, but I left it at a home near the first river and continued on foot. After wading the river, I walked to the second river a mile away. After wading the second river, I continued on another two miles to Waipia. The trek was a hot one. The forest had been cleared for a hundred yards on either side of the dirt road. You walked without shade in that humid tropical island.

Often I would chuckle to myself about God having a sense of humor. He didn't send me to Seram when I was young, and such treks would have been easier. He waited till I was nearly fifty. I don't like boats, so He sent me to an island province where travel by boat is all there is. I don't like boney fishy-tasting fish, He sent me where boney fishy-tasting fish is the staple diet.

Soon after leaving the Masohi area, before the first river, you pass a village of primitive tribals. They formerly lived in the forest, but the government bought their land and moved them to a simple government housing location near Masohi. They still lived by hunting wildlife and gathering edible vegetation in the forest. From time to time, I would meet some of them at one of the two rivers. We could barely communicate with hand signs and the limited Indonesian language they could understand. They had their own tribal language.

One trip, I saw a place between the two rivers, where someone had started clearing a plot of forest for planting. On my next trip, the clearing had stopped, and there were signs warning, "Death to anyone who clears this land." There were also arrows hanging from branches and red-dye handprints on the tree trunks. The primitives were peaceful, provided no one encroached on their land.

I would spend four or five days in Waipia. I walked many miles, visiting the people, conducting Bible studies, or worship services, etc. I rented a small simple wooden house, constructed of very thin plywood walls (outer walls, no inner walls), plywood windows, cement floors in the living room and both bedrooms. The kitchen and dining areas had a dirt floor. It had a tin roof, which leaked here and there. It was adequate for my short-term needs. The backyard provided a water well, a simple outhouse, and a simple enclosure in which to bathe. However, in the dry season, we bathed after dark, with one bucket of water, while standing over vegetable plants so they could get watered daily.

At night, I was never lonely; a small bat slept hanging from the rafter over the foot of my bed—at least it was usually there when I woke up each morning.

Church members in Waipia took turns providing meals for me, either in their house or mine. During the long dry season, when the wells went dry, they had to walk back to the river to get water. Someone did that for me, allowing me to have more time for visitation and ministry opportunities.

After four or five days in Waipia, I packed up for the trek back to Masohi. The rivers tended to flood for my return trips. The river bottom was football-shaped rocks, which shifted as you stepped on them, making balancing difficult. If the river rose, the raging water became frightening. On one trip back, just a few days prior to a furlough, the river was high-chest deep and violent. I was terrified and unable (physically or emotionally) to wade across alone. Finally, several young men crossed from the other side; I swallowed my pride asked for help.

They walked me one hundred yards upstream, then two guys took my backpack, two guys held my hands and others just accompanied us. We jumped in and jumped up and down, allowing the swift current to carry us both downstream and across the river. They made it look easy and fun as well. However, if someone was swept past the safe crossing area, death was a possibility by drowning or by being eaten by saltwater crocodiles where the river met the sea.

On another trip back to Masohi, at the height of the hot dry season, I experienced heat exhaustion. When I finally reached Masohi and the home of Pak Stev, I sat down and could not get up for several hours. That was kind of frightening too.

I usually stayed in Masohi one or two nights before going on to the harbor to catch a people ferry for my return to Ambon. In Masohi, I made visits, taught Bible studies, and led worship.

During trips to Seram, I usually did not feel tired until I arrived back home in Ambon, but then I was exhausted. I always joked to Linda, "It is so good to be home with my own potty (not a squatty), my own bed (not a woven mat on top of boards), with my own wife." Linda never questioned "my own potty" and "my own bed," but always asked, "And whose wife have you been with?" *Without laughter, there would have been times we could not made it.*

When we agreed to move from Java to Ambon, we knew the govern-ment red tape would be far worse than any we had experienced before. The province of Maluku was given special and tight oversight by the central government. That was because after the defeat of Japan in WW II, the Dutch colonial government tried to reestablish itself in Indonesia. The Indonesians fought and won a revolutionary war against Holland and became an independent republic on August 17, 1947.

The people of Maluku, however, has sided with the Dutch, not the revolutionary forces. So now, forty years later, the central government still didn't fully trust the people of Maluku. (Perhaps not very differ-ent from the way the U.S. government viewed the southern states after the American Civil War.) The government was also highly sus-picious of Westerners wanting to live and work in Maluku. Thus the extraordinary red tape for us to get settled in Maluku.

For that reason, we moved to Ambon prior to taking our nor-mal home leave. I chose that so we could "jump through all the government hoops" to establish ourselves as residents then return to the States for six months. That enabled us to return to Ambon after furlough and hit the ground running in regard to our work. It was somewhat awkward, but in the end, the plan worked out for the best. Of course, the people at church were disappointed that we took a six month furlough so soon after moving to Ambon. It was somewhat awkward, but it was best.

We were assigned to Ambon to facilitate evangelism, church planting, and to develop local spiritual leadership. Although the assignment was for the whole province of Maluku, we were to begin by assisting the pastors of the Ambon and Waipia churches. Of course, our task must be accomplished without overshadowing or supplanting the leadership of those pastors.

Both congregations had existed for about three years. Each had a pastor from Java. Each congregation was financially dependent on their sponsoring church (two different Jakarta churches), and little, if any, progress was being made to reverse that dependency or to develop local leadership.

The pastor of the Ambon congregation was an Ambonese born and raised in Jakarta. He was a new graduate of the Baptist seminary. The pastor of the Waipia congregation was Javanese, thus though he was Indonesian, he was a foreigner in Seram, but not as foreign as me. I often referred to him as a real live missionary. He previously pastored a small congregation in a small city in Central Java. He did not have a seminary degree but had completed a number of courses through the extension program of the Baptist seminary. Actually, I had taught him two of his courses during the year (1974–75) we lived in the Worten home in Purwokerto.

While we were on our six-month home leave, taken after working through the government red tape mentioned above, the sponsoring church of the Ambon church purchased a plot of land with a small run-down wooden house in suburbs of Ambon. The house was divided into three small rooms, separated by woven bamboo walls and had a rusty tin roof. Much of the land seemed unusable since the back third of the property sloped down steeply to the rear.

When we returned from the USA, the church had about a year left on the leased building it had used since the church began. Thus the newly purchased property meant the sponsoring church would not make another multiyear lease on the building presently used for the church.

The Ambon congregation was not pleased with the new property, which had been purchased without any input from them. But as an old saying says, "Beggars can't be choosy." Linda and I informally started a "building fund" by quietly making small monthly donations designated for that purpose. After a few months, others joined us. As the "building fund" slowly grew, contributions grew also.

The Ambon pastor was a good, though inexperienced, pastor. He did a good job at preaching, but lacked some people skills and didn't seem able to develop lay leadership. Thus I was asked, by both the pastor and the sponsoring church, to conduct seminary extension classes, as well as other training opportunities to develop local leadership. During our time in Ambon, we saw significant measurable progress in the church. However, in my estimation, Linda (not the pastor or I) had the most significant role in the maturing of the Ambon church.

The members were discouraged about the land and old house purchased for a place of worship. We finally had a workday to clean up the property and evaluate what could be done with the building. Another workday was scheduled the following week. For that workday, Linda took a big pot of red beans and rice. The food was well received. On ensuing workdays, other ladies brought or sent food as well.

Hope and excitement began to slowly displace discouragement about the new property. Workdays became "work and fellowship days." Unity began to grow among the membership, which included four ethnic groups. *Slowly, the congregation began to develop as a body with purpose.* The group, which just assembled to worship, *was beginning to see itself as the body of Christ.* It all seemed to start with Linda's pot of beans and rice.

Financial matters of the Ambon church were in a mess. Although the church voted on a budget, its spending seemed to have little relationship with their budget. There was no misuse of funds, rather a propensity to vote to do something that was not budgeted or purchase something that was not budgeted. Then when a bill for a budgeted item arrived (i.e., to pay for church literature, the electric bill, etc.), there might not be sufficient funds to pay the bill. Members were often asked to give special offerings to meet those cash shortages. Church business meetings took over two hours. Money problems were always a hot topic, and the discussion went on and on. *Finally, in desperation, the congregation asked Linda to become the church treasurer.*

Linda accepted their request, on condition she be authorized to change their system of bookkeeping to a double-entry system and change how money was handled and spent. She also told the congregation that a bank account must be opened, a minimum amount of petty cash must be kept by the treasurer, and a finance committee must be selected.

The members of the finance committee would be required to be trained by Linda to understand the new bookkeeping system, how to audit the books and reconcile the books with the bank statement and petty cash. That audit and reconciliation would be done monthly by the committee and treasurer. A monthly written financial report must be given to the church. She further stated that she would be treasurer for two years, then the church would elect a new treasurer from within the trained finance committee. *Drastic situations often call for drastic* (but sound) *measures.*

Linda used the double-entry bookkeeping used by our Baptist Mission. *The first few business meetings proved to be a steep learning curve for the congregation. After that, the people began to feel excitement about the future.* They felt that their money problems would be solved and that items in the budget would be funded without repetitive special offerings. The level of giving began to grow month by month.

Within a year, the congregation began to believe that continued financial dependency on the sponsoring church was no longer necessary. The building fund also began to grow far beyond expectations. The openness and stabilization of church finances was transformative for the Ambon congregation.

A year and half after our arrival in Ambon, the Waipia pastor resigned and returned to Java to study in the campus program of the Baptist seminary. The sponsoring church, asked me to give general oversight to the Waipia church and to train local lay leaders through seminary extension classes. I began teaching them every third week, during my trips to Waipia (described earlier). I also carried out duties of a part-time interim pastor on those trips.

The Waipia congregation made some good progress, but lacked mature spiritual lay leadership. They began a building program; however, they depended on their sponsoring church to raise the money for their new building. Pride may have been the root of their problem. They desired a very substantial brick building—much larger than projected needs. Had they settled for a wooden building, like their homes, they would more likely have able to raise funds themselves, without needing help from outside.

The fellowship in Masohi, Seram, also grew and bought their own building, even though they did not have a regular pastor. Their members, however, were more mature spiritually and also had better paying jobs than the congregation in Waipia.

We had begun to penetrate a few new areas on the islands of Ambon and Seram when we were forced to leave Indonesia in 1990.

Dark Days in Ambon

Renewing missionary visas (permission to live and work in Indonesia) was always a lengthy hassle. However, during the fall of 1989, we experienced exceptional difficulties. Four-month delays were the norm, but after six months and no word (in spite of numerous inquiries by our Jakarta office) *the police in Ambon put us under (real, although unofficial) "island arrest." The police were friendly but had to cover their own backs.* We were completely free on Ambon but could not leave our island. That ended our trips to Seram, or anywhere else.

Matt had a nine-day break for Easter in 1990. He could not come home, or the police would not allow him to return to school, due to lack of visa renewal. During that time, Linda's only sibling had a stroke, and Linda would not have been able to return for a funeral, had her sister died. *It was a stressful five months of "island arrest."*

During this time, we were also trying to deal with a long-term unresolved family issue. Linda and I were being crushed by that persistent issue that nearly sucked the lifeblood out of us, as were others involved with the issue.

In the midst of those and other trials, I received a letter from an old pen pal. It is normal for missionaries to receive simple but sincere letters of encouragement from children, who study about missions and missionaries. Most letters are written by girls between the age of nine and twelve, who share our birthday. Most only wrote once; however, sometimes I would receive more than one letter over a period of two or three years. I tried to answer most of those letters, answering their questions and sharing a little about our work.

Vicki Helton, a ten-year-old girl in Belmont, North Carolina, had written me at least two times, beginning in mid-1970, our first year in Indonesia.

In my first response to Vicki, I mentioned, "On your birthday have an extra bowl of ice cream for me. We cannot buy ice cream where we live." After her next birthday, *she wrote again* saying that "at the family party, her mom decorated a cupcake and put a bowl of ice cream beside it, proclaiming, *"This cup cake and ice cream is for Fred."*

Now, twenty years later, I received another letter from Vicki. She explained that she recently learned how to find our address and was excited to learn that we were still in Indonesia. She explained that she was now a mother and the wife of a rural pastor in southwest North Carolina. She said, after she got married, she continued her mother's tradition of setting aside a cupcake and a bowl of ice cream for Fred. Furthermore, Vicki explained that she "had carefully preserved my letters and still uses them in opportunities to tell others about missionaries."

Before I finished reading Vicki's letter, it was spotted with teardrops. I laid her letter down and cried. *Thus, during my second most trying time abroad, God moved an old pen pal to reconnect with me and write an encouraging letter, when I most needed it.*

The Lord reminded me, in a tangible way, that He had our back. We could trust Him and continue to walk in faith, even without our understanding of where He was leading. Many say God had nothing to do with events like that; it was just coincidence. Yes, *it may look like coincidence to some; however, often that which appears to be mere coincidence is, instead, God working incognito.*

In late May 1990, I finally received police permission to fly to Jakarta to make a last-ditch effort to acquire a visa renewal. My efforts failed, but while there, Charles Cole said, "Fred, 'holding on' is not always a 'sign of faith.' Sometimes it can be a 'sign of lack of faith.'" It was as if God had spoken through Charles, and I was suddenly at peace. Later, Charles could not understand why we left

Indonesia, or that he had unknowingly given me God's permission to leave.

Many years later, after retirement, Linda and I visited Charles and Barbara in their home near Shreveport, Louisiana. As we chatted, I told Charles how God had used him to help me discern God's will in that matter. I think Charles and Barbara finally understood.

Good-Bye, Indonesia

O ur Jakarta office purchased one-way tickets to the USA for the three of us. We were booked to board Garuda Indonesian Airlines in Biak, an island near Irian Jaya (Indonesian New Guinea). Matt would meet us in Biak on the day of our departure to the USA. I returned to Ambon; we packed our suitcases, closed up our house and belongings, and departed Ambon on May 31, 1990.

Linda and I arrived in Biak a day before Matt. *So we were able to visit a huge cave where Japanese soldiers hid during WWII. We were also taken up into the hills to see the location of General Douglas McArthur's WW II hilltop base in Biak, after he was forced to flee the Philippines. I picked up a rock as a remembrance.*

We stayed the night in a simple missionary guesthouse, and the following day, Matt caught a missionary flight (not without several problems, which I won't go into) and flew to Biak to join us, just in time to catch our flight to Los Angeles. On the first of June 1990, we departed Indonesia on an "exit only permit," which meant we gave up our visa to Indonesia.

We were brokenhearted about being "politely" forced to leave Indonesia, a country and work we loved and enjoyed for twenty years, where three of our children had grown into young adulthood, and where our fourth was born. Nonetheless, we were at peace, though we had no idea what God had in store for our future. We would, however, discover His plans during nearly a month in the USA.

Actually, a year earlier, we had discussed our situation with Jerry Rankin, then serving as director to the South & Southeast Asia Area, for the International Mission Board. He had offered two possibilities, if we were forced to leave Indonesia. The first was in Australia, the second in the Philippines. However, neither of those fit our gifts or interest, nor did we feel leadership from God. Now a year later, we had departed Indonesia and had no place to serve.

On the other hand, for two years, I had a burden for three couples (Clyde and Elaine Meador, Jim and Carolyn McAtee, and Von and Marge Worten), who formerly served in Indonesia but, due to loss of visas in 1988, had transferred to a new kind of work on the Indian subcontinent. They were living what I imagined to be an impossible lifestyle.

I had begun to pray daily for those couples and wrote letters of encouragement to them. That was part of the stress I felt during our 1988 furlough, which I mentioned earlier. These dear friends had become itinerant missionaries; without a home, living out of their suitcases for months at a time, moving to a different location every week in order to give short-term training to unschooled pastors all across India.

After "the team" conducted training for all their scheduled groups, they began the rotation all over again. Men not used to classrooms sat on the floor for nearly eight hours a day for five days, soaking up all the missionaries taught them. Then they returned home to continue serving their church. Six months later, they were back for another week of training (again and again).

Some say that "prayer changes things"; however prayer also changes the heart of the "pray-er" (the person who prays). By then my burden for my missionary friends had expanded to include those Indian lay pastors serving without formal training, probably feeling very lonely, without much camaraderie. Thus the Lord began to lay a new burden on me—a burden for the country I had not wanted to even fly over much less visit or work in. Talk about prejudice ... wow! and I called myself a follower of Jesus?

I was not to the place that I was willing to make a long-term commitment to India. Besides, Linda and I were still hopeful of being able to return to Indonesia. So we went back to Jerry Rankin—this time by phone. "We have eighteen months left before we furlough again, how about letting us serve with *SAPIM (South Asia and Pacific Itinerant Mission)* until furlough," I said. "Then maybe the door to Indonesia will reopen."

Upon hearing me try to barter with him (the Indonesia way), I imagine Dr. Rankin chuckled under his breath before agreeing with my offer. While still serving in Indonesia, Jerry had also done part-time work in India beginning in 1979. That work was similar to what SAPIM was now doing full-time. Thus Jerry's early work in India was a precursor of SAPIM (more details about that later). He also knew us well enough to know that if we served in India for eighteen months, we would be hooked. So he graciously "gave in" and said, "OK."

We Joined the IMB-SAPIM Team

During our brief vacation in the States, we visited our children, Linda's sister, my dad and purchased new luggage and a few other things we would need for our new homeless itinerant ministry and lifestyle.

Near the end of June 1990, Linda, Matt, and I flew back to Indonesia on a tourist visa to attend the annual SAPIM Mission Meeting. That year, it was held at the same time and place as the Indonesian Mission Meeting. Matt was back with MK friends, and we were among friends too. We could fellowship with missionaries still serving in Indonesia, and we became the fourth ex-Indonesia couple (Becks, Meadors, McAtees, and Wortens) with SAPIM. The eight of us, along with Hugh and Katheryn Smith, ex-Malaysia missionaries, made up the SAPIM Mission. There were five couples; we needed a minimum of six couples. Later, that minimum number increased as the scope of work enlarged.

Linda and I learned what a one-year schedule looked like. It was broken into two six-month segments; the first was very specific revealing where each SAPIM couple would be every day, what each would be doing, what subjects they would be teaching, etc. The schedule also included transportation instructions and where we'd sleep each night—in a church, guesthouse, small hotel, etc.

During that meeting, new writing assignments were divided among us. I was asked to write the textbook for *Developing Leaders for the Local Church*. It would be taught to pastors in eighteen months. I was given a schedule to turn in three rough draft copies in February 1991, less than eight months away.

I was not a writer. We would be on the road for the next six months, and I would be away from my personal library. Fortunately, I would spend four months in India prior to actually writing my rough draft. Those months in India ensured a very basic understanding of leadership needs in both large and small churches, in both city and rural locations.

In February '91, the rough drafts would be read by my boss and two SAPIM peers. They would make suggestions of needed changes or additions. Then I would have a month to revise the book and send it to our office in Bangalore, India. There it would be translated into about twelve Indian languages, printed by photocopy, put into a spiral binder, then given to the pastors who attended our seminars.

Thinking about it now, still makes me breathless. More about that later. Yes, others were given writing assignments on other basic subjects. Two years later, I was asked to write a second book, *Church Administration*. Books, on SAPIM curriculum subjects would be the only library many participating pastors would own. Some of SAPIMs other books/courses were *Church Planting, How to Teach the Bible, Spiritual Warfare, Sermon Preparation, Spiritual Disciplines, The Doctrine of God, The Doctrine of Salvation, Baptist Distinctives and History*, and many more.

Following SAPIM meeting, we took Matt to Penang, Malaysia, to enroll in Dalat School for his sophomore year of high school. He would live in a rented house improvised into a coed dorm. Leslie and Edna Smith had been dorm parents for our three older kids in Jakarta. They were delaying their retirement for two years, to get this "off campus" Baptist dorm started. Matt's experiences with three boarding schools were mainly good, as were our older children's experiences in Jakarta, Indonesia.

After our first semester in India, Linda, Matt, and I were able to return (as tourists) to our rented home in Ambon, Indonesia, for the Christmas holidays. I read a lot and made notes to be used to write my assigned book, *Developing Leaders for Local Churches*. Movers packed and shipped our belongings to Jakarta for storage.

In mid-January 1991, we left Ambon for good. We flew to Malaysia, where we would do rural training seminars and other ministries for a month. We worked most of the day then returned to a guesthouse in town. After dinner, I worked late into the night writing the manuscript of my book. The following evening, Linda typed my handwritten notes into the computer while I wrote more. By the end of the month, the two of us finished the rough draft on schedule.

In mid-February, we flew to Luzon, Philippines, for a huge conference on church planting that was arranged by Jerry Rankin, our area director. Copies of my book were taken by Clyde and two SAPIM peers to read and critique. After another month, I had their marked copies and revised the book to include their suggested cuts and additions. The finished book, only about fifty pages of simplified English, was translated into a dozen languages of India.

From Luzon, SAPIM couples flew south to Mindanao. We spent a week experiencing a sustainable agriculture program created by IMB Missionary Harold Watson. It was so good that Herold was awarded the top medal given by the Philippine President, along with a cash award.

I did not know it then, but Clyde had plans to begin a scaled-down version of that program in the Indian State of Orissa. Two years later (1993), missionary journeyman (two-year appointment), John Langston began a "BOOST Project" (Baptist Out of School Training) to open our agriculture work in Orissa. After two years, Calvin and Margaret Fox, seasoned agriculture missionaries, moved from the Philippine project to continue and enlarge the Orissa project. That ministry became a hub for training farmers, church planters, and pastors in "off season food and cash crops" and in "chronological Bible storying" (more details later).

Dr. Clyde Meador was SAPIM director. He walks daily with the Lord and is gifted with leadership, management, and people skills beyond my ability to fathom. Clyde's wife, Elaine, is a perfect complement to Clyde's leadership skills. Little did I realize that two years later, I would be asked to fill Clyde's shoes, as SAPIM director and director of SBC work in India. Clyde moved to Singapore to become area director for South and Southeast Asia (thus still my boss), after Jerry Rankin returned to the States to become IMB president.

Eleven years later, in August 2001, as Linda and I were leaving the field for our final furlough (Stateside assignment) before retirement, Clyde was moving to Richmond, Virginia, to eventually become executive vice president at IMB. Clyde is one of the most influential people in my life. He gave me opportunities to take on assignments that I would never have dreamed of doing. He patiently mentored me through all of the difficult tasks he gave me. Clyde is a dear friend who pours his life into others, making them better people to the glory of God.

Back to the chronology of preparing to enter India for the first time. After getting Matt settled into Dalat School (summer 1990), Linda and I joined Jim and Carolyn McAtee for two weeks in a cottage in the Cameron Highlands of Malaysia. It was a time of intensive preparation to teach three courses a day for a week to lay pastors who would attend our training seminars. During the next four months, we would be teaching, fourteen different, weeklong seminars in twelve different languages in ten different states of India and two states of Pakistan. Local translators were a necessity.

Working through a translator is hard work. We must structure our thoughts and sentences so the translator can quickly follow our thought pattern, quickly translate our teaching, to enable our students to understand our intent as well as the importance of what is taught. It is three-way communication: (1) We teach the people through the translator. (2) The translator seeks to communicate what we say and hopefully the meaning of what we say. (3) Then the listeners communicate back to the teacher verbally or through body language that they understand or don't understand. *If the learners don't understand, either the teacher or the translator, or both of them, must make major adjustments.*

After our preparations in Malaysia, the McAtees and Becks flew to Bangkok, Thailand, to apply for "five-month tourist visas" to enter India. While in Bangkok, we stayed in the Meadors' apartment while they were out of town. Beyond the tension of the visa process (India did not give a visa for missionary work), it was a relaxing week. *We would accompany the McAtees into and throughout our first four months in India and a month in Pakistan. We would learn the ropes from them. They would orient us to country, customs, and work. A week later, the needed visas were in our passports.*

Part of SAPIM strategy was to send two couples into India for up to five months. Both couples would travel and teach each training seminar together. That provided both fellowship and backup for the four missionaries. It also modeled diversity of teaching styles for the trainees. While two couples worked in India, other couples worked in the other smaller countries of South Asia (Pakistan, Bangladesh, Nepal, and Sri Lanka). Bhutan and the Maldives, also in South Asia, would require extraordinary creative efforts.

As we eventually added other couples to SAPIM, we doubled the number of seminar locations in India and added East Malaysia (North Borneo), Burma, and a Burmese refugee camp in Thailand to our training cycle. We also made a strategic change in our seminar content. We reduced the number of SAPIM curriculum courses taught from three to two. We replaced the dropped course with an expository study of select books of the Bible each seminar.

SIDE NOTE: In the above mentioned Burmese refugee camp, out from Mae Sod, Thailand, Thra (Rev) Simon founded the Kawthoolei Karen Baptist Church and Bible College. On our first trip to teach in that Bible college, students sang Handel's "Hallelujah Chorus" without musical accompaniment. It was the most beautiful I have heard. They performed in a simple bamboo building with a straw roof and dirt floor. However, the point of this "side note" is that two of those young students (now married), Rainbow and Esther Gold, now serve as pastor and wife of the Karen Burmese Congregation, of FBC, Amarillo, Texas. Small world!

After couples completed a semester in India, they would switch over to the non-India locations for the next semester and vice versa. That flip-flopping enabled us to continually gain entrance into countries that did not issue visas to permanent missionaries. As seminars increased, we sent four couples, or more, to India each semester.

Into India and the Entire Subcontinent

As we were about to enter India for the first time, *my thoughts wandered back to a missionary hero.* In *1793, William Carey* (1761–1834) a cobbler and a pastor, became the first British Baptist missionary to India. There were other Christian missionaries there before Carey, but Carey is known as "father of the modern missionary movement." I will not say much about Carey's ministries here, but more should read that phenomenal man's missionary story.

Later, on our first trip to Calcutta/Kolkata, we attended worship at one of the churches Carey established. I don't recall its original name, but after his death, it was renamed Carey Baptist Church. A few pieces of original furniture are still in the building. The baptistery is built into the floor and is covered by thick wide wooden planks. American, Adoniram Judson, then aged twenty-five, and his wife, Ann (Hassel) were baptized in that baptistery. They were en route to Burma, where they served for almost forty years. Luther Rice was also baptized with the Judsons. I was told that Corrie ten Boom was also baptized in Carey Baptist Church, after WWII.

While in Calcutta/Kolkata, the McAtees took us on an excursion, by taxi, to Serampore, to see the college Carey established. We also visited the Carey Museum and the cemetery where Carey and many family members are buried. A large sandstone slab, which was cracked, covered Carey's grave. It was inscribed "Here lies Carey the worm." That inscription was Carey's wish.

In 1993, IMB promoted revival meetings in Indian Baptist Churches all across India, with American volunteers participating in those revival efforts. Dr. Meador invited representatives from every Baptist group in India, to gather in Calcutta to celebrate the *two hundredth anniversary of William Carey's 1793 arrival in India.* A huge tent was rented and placed on the grounds of a large hotel. One thousand one hundred Baptist pastors and leaders attended from all over India. I believe it was the first such meeting of Baptists of every stripe and from every state. Most people do not realize that Baptists in India are only outnumbered by the number of Baptists in the USA.

Dr. Meador invited Rev. Karl Saragih, from Indonesia, to be the special Bible teacher. He spoke on the "Pastors' Spiritual Ministries," and he rang everyone's bell. I was introduced as the new director of IMB work in India and was kept busy for two days with personal interviews with more Baptist leaders than I could count. Several new partnerships developed from those interviews.

William Carey's motto was "ATTEMPT GREAT THINGS FOR GOD. EXPECT GREAT THINGS FROM GOD." I like his motto, but borrowed Carey's "model" and gave it a new twist. "EXPECT GREAT THINGS FROM GOD'S PEOPLE; ATTEMPT GREAT THINGS THROUGH GOD'S PEOPLE." I usually included my motto on the bottom of letters to Indian Baptist leaders. I also used it in many of my "newsletters" home.

Several years later, I made *a second trip to Serampore* because a guest requested to see it. We were graciously received by Dr. J. T. K. Daniel, principal of Serampore College. Dr. Daniel even invited us to see his on-campus apartment, the same apartment Carey occupied as principal. He then took us to the adjoining apartment where Dr. Carey died. Indians tend to be very gracious.

One last Carey side story: Most of present-day Indonesia was colonized first by the Dutch East India Company (VOC) 1602–1799. Then by the Dutch government, as the Dutch East Indies, 1799–1942. Columbus was seeking a shorter sea route to those Indies when he bumped into the New World/North America.

There was, however, a short British Interlude in Ambon (1806–1815) and the Molucca Islands. During that British Interlude, *Carey's third son, Jabez Carey,* served the British colonial government as minister of education. In 1815, *Ambon (where we served 1985–1990) was given back to the Dutch, in exchange for land in Sumatra.* It is interesting that whether we realize it or not, history crosses all of our paths—sometimes multiple times.

I could write more about Carey, but most people would enjoy reading that phenomenal man's missionary story for themselves.

Back to entering India for the first time. We had an evening flight from Bangkok, Thailand, to Mumbai (Bombay), India, arriving after midnight, in mid-August 1990. An hour after landing, we cleared Immigration and claimed our luggage. We rented two taxis to the Tunga Paradise Hotel, a small hotel not far from the airport. After a short night of rest, we were back at the airport for an early morning fight to Bangalore, the flower city of India. Bangalore's mild climate provided a pleasant location for our India office and guesthouse, next door to the Baptist Hospital.

We had just over a week to make final preparations for a semester of teaching throughout India. Our preparations included outfitting ourselves with proper clothing. The men had it easy because many Indian men wear Western attire. However, in Pakistan, our men wore Pakistani attire, like all Pakistani men.

The ladies, however, were expected to dress in the non-Western attire of most Indian ladies. Carolyn already had her Indian wardrobe, Linda purchased material and gave it to a tailor to have "sarees" and "salwar kameez" outfits made. She wore them nearly 100 percent of the time that she was in either India, Pakistan, Bangladesh, or Sri Lanka. She was very beautiful in them. She always flew into and out of India wearing Western clothes; we were tourists.

In Bangalore, Mrs. Florence Charles, and later, Mrs. Nirmala Kumar, our office manager, ordered Indian air and train tickets for the semester. Hotel or guesthouse reservations were also made, and SAPIM books were sent to seminar locations. Our hotels were adequate, although there are varying degrees of adequacy. We usually rated our hotels by moons, not stars. There are some four- and five-star hotels in India. Although we did not stay in them, we did occasionally enjoy a change of pace meal in the restaurant of a four-star hotel.

In Mumbai (Bombay), SAPIM worked with NIM through Rev. Krupananda Gollapalli and later through Pastor Vivian Fernandes for a few weeks each semester. That work was mostly in a metropolitan context. Brother Vivian is the present leader of the fast-growing Convention of Baptist Churches of Maharashtra. *That work, as well as some new work in Calcutta and Orissa, was begun by Dr. Owen Cooper, a Baptist businessman from Mississippi.* Dr. Cooper built several factories in India and made frequent business trips to his factories.

Mr. Cooper, was concerned with "lost-ness" in India. He established Universal Concern, in order to hire Indian church planters to evangelize and plant churches. Mr. Cooper was also the last layman to be elected president of the Southern Baptist Convention. Perhaps we need more laymen serving as SBC president. In 1981, Dr. Cooper asked the International Mission Board, SBC, to assume the work he had begun in India. I think Dr. Keith Parks (another former Indonesia missionary), then president of IMB, accepted that challenge from Dr. Cooper.

IMB established NIM (National Indian Ministries) to administer work begun by Owen Cooper. Dr. Bill Wakefield asked Jerry and Bobbye Rankin, then missionaries to Indonesia, to make periodic trips to India. They were to conduct short-term training for those young Indian churches and continue facilitating church planting growth. Rankin also enlisted help from several Malaysia-based missionaries, especially Jack Shelby and Bob & Marge Wakefield, to join him in that short-term training.

Eventually, the Rankins transferred from Indonesia to give greater attention to India. Rankin asked Reverend Krupananda of Karnataka to move to Mumbai to serve as national director of NIM. IMB purchased two flats in Andheri (suburb of Bombay), as an NIM office and a guesthouse.

Dr. Rankin mentioned that he encountered two persistent short-term training problems. First, borrowing different missionary trainers from other countries lacked consistency. Secondly, enlisting pastors from America presented multiple logistical problems. It was also difficult for those American pastors to present culturally appropriate material. It was also hard for them to simplify their teaching for pastors with minimal education.

Both of those problems disappeared in 1988. Many missionary couples in Indonesia lost their missionary visa and transferred to other countries. Several of those couples chose to continue the itinerant training begun by Rankin and others. The big difference was that those couples would be full-time trainers. Jerry Rankin asked Clyde Meador to direct IMB work in India, because Jerry had been given administrative duties in Singapore for the entire region. Thus, the Meadors, McAtees, and Wortens from Indonesia, as well as Hugh and Katheryn Smith from Malaysia created SAPIM (South Asia and Pacific Itinerant Mission). *Linda and I joined SAPIM about eighteen months later (June 1990).*

The Mumbai (Bombay) megacity work has spread throughout many rural districts of the state. The work in Orissa started and continued in a rural context, but has spread to cities as well. The work in West Bengal (Calcutta/Kolkata and some rural areas) had special challenges and we eventually lessened our role there.

FLASHBACK: In the mid-1960s, IMB/SBC was able to obtain visas to India for Dr. and Mrs. Jasper McPhail, a cardiovascular surgeon. He would work at the Vellore Christian Medical Center, in Tamil Nadu. Later, he was able to register the IMB for approved medical work. McPhail purchased land in Bangalore where he established a clinic, in an abandoned chicken coop. In 1968, he opened the first phase of the Bangalore Baptist Hospital, after other medical staff received visas. The hospital staff began to establish churches, and the Indian Baptist Mission (organization of Southern Baptist missionaries in a country) was created.

The Indian Baptist Mission began to hire national pastors/evangelists to do follow-up on the Hospital ministries and start churches. The salaries of those church workers and the church buildings were heavily subsidized by the Mission's budget. The first ten years of that program, only produced 21 churches, even though a great environment for church growth existed. The lack of growth was due in part to limited Mission budgets, which inhibited hiring more pastors/ evangelists. However, the larger problem was a non-indigenous strategy. We had dwealt with a similar situation about relying on subsidy, in Indonesia in 1971.

Therefore, it was very appropriate for someone like Jerry Rankin, a church planter in Indonesia, to be asked to go to India for several months in 1979, to assess the India situation. After the assessment. Rankin was to give appropriate training about viable church planting strategies to the medical missionaries and the hired national workers. Subsidies were phased out and a new strategy of indigenous approaches of discipleship training, house churches and lay leaders.

Indigenous means *native to the area*, where growth is normal, not forced or propped up by subsidies. Regarding that, I have a saying, "*How you begin is what you achieve in the end.*" A subsidy is only good, if it encourages local initiative, without causing local dependency.

The next ten years, after Rankin's visit, the number of churches grew from 21 to 440. The changes Rankin introduced made a big difference.

Dr. Rankin has stated that from that success, "a vision began to emerge to launch similar training in partnership with other Baptist groups throughout India." In the mid-1980's, when most IMB medical missionaries left, the organization changed its name to the Indian Baptist Society (IBS). After that, for many years, Dr. Rebekah Naylor was the only IMB missionary with a missionary visa for India. However, beginning in 1988, there was a constantly growing number of our people there without missionary visas.

SAPIM worked in Bangalore and throughout Karnataka in collaboration with Dr. Rebekah Naylor of the Baptist Hospital, as well as with Reverend Divaker and later Reverend A. Jacob (Church Development Department, IBS). That IBS work continues its remarkable growth throughout the state today. On October 18, 2016, "Dr.

Rebekah A Naylor was awarded the 2016 Surgical Humanitarian Award, by the American College of Surgeons, for her many years of services to the medically underserved in India (1973-2002).

Between 1992 and 1998, additional missionaries began to slowly transfer to SAPIM as the work grew. Several of those couples had previously served in Indonesia: Ray and Joyce Rogers, Tom and Hazel Barron, Harry and Barbara Bush, and eventually Johnny and Diana Norwood, as well as several non-Indonesia missionaries. We also borrowed Hal and Carol Jacks for six weeks each year. The Jacks formerly served in Indonesia but were then in Sri Lanka.

In 1993, my role underwent drastic change. Dr. Rankin became president of IMB and moved to Richmond, Virginia. Dr. Clyde Meador moved into Rankin's previous job, as area/regional director. Thus in addition to teaching training seminars, I became the director of SAPIM. That was a steep learning curve, made more difficult because I also became director of IMB work in India. Those tasks seemed overwhelming, but also afforded unbelievable opportunities. I would be stretched beyond my imagination. Linda was my indispensable helper and encourager, and Clyde Meador mentored me through it all.

My new job was "bigger than me"—a "little man" in a "big position." Would I be a small-thinking leader, mishandle great opportunities, and make our personnel miserable in the process? Or would I allow God to equip me and work through me, to equip and enable both national and missionary peers to accomplish greater things? Human assessment of my success or failure is not mine to make; only the people I led can objectively make that evaluation. I would assume some mixed evaluations. Of course, our Heavenly Father is the ultimate judge.

A couple of years later, in 1995, the IMB trustees approved my appointment as associate to the area director, which broadened my scope of responsibility to all of South Asia (India, Pakistan, Nepal, Bhutan, Bangladesh, Sri Lanka, and the Maldives). I no longer had the luxury of teaching in SAPIM seminars.

In 1995, Jim and Carolyn McAtee transferred from SAPIM to fill a needed role as "strategy coordinators" for the country of Myanmar (Burma), where Baptist missionary Adiniram Judson served, overlapping part of the time frame of William Carey, in India. The McAtees enlisted SAPIM and others to come in periodically to help him. Linda and I made one trip to Myanmar and taught with the McAtees in three weeklong training seminars, with three different Baptist groups in and near Yangon (Rangoon).

In 1998, because of increasing workload, I transferred the administration of SAPIM to Harry and Barbara Bush. They became co-directors of SAPIM, and the work continued to expand and flourish under their leadership. An IMB field reorganization brought about a name change; "SAPIM" became "LEAD" (Leadership, Equipping, and Development). Thus Linda and I were no longer members of SAPIM/LEAD, but that ministry still fell within my overall responsibilities as associate to the area/regional director/leader.

In 2016, (fourteen years after our retirement), continued increases of personnel in South Asia enabled our localized IMB personnel to assume training duties for the people they served. They would also be able to spend more time developing local trainers from among their people. That was good but meant there was no longer a need for an itinerant training team. For twenty-eight years, it had been a much-needed and very productive ministry, but we must change with the times. In the end, SAPIM/LEAD went the way of the horse and buggy. I have no regrets; however, I rejoice that Linda and I had the privilege of being a part of SAPIM's early days and well into its heyday.

The majority of Baptist work in India did not originate with IMB. It was the result of many different foreign and local Baptist entities, associations, or conventions throughout that vast country. British Baptists, American Baptists, Canadian Baptists, Swedish Baptists, Conservative Baptists and others, including many local spinoffs, were the "founders." Most missionaries of above-named foreign groups seemed to have departed from India by the mid-

1950s. IMB/SBC, the new kid on the block, was just getting started in India.

You may wonder if there are other denominations in India, because I have only mentioned Baptists. Yes, there are many denominations in India, However, my story deals with working with Baptists.

The Roman Catholic church is the overall largest denomination in India. There are, of course, Pentecostal churches and others. The two dominant Protestant denominations are the Church of North India (CNI) and the Church of South India (CSI). They were both established in the midtwentieth century by uniting several Protestant denominations of varying doctrines and polity, including the Anglicans, Methodists, Presbyterians, etc.

My assumption is the CSI and CNI were the result of the ecumenical movement of midtwentieth century, as well as the departure of great numbers of foreign Protestant missionaries.

A number of Baptist churches, especially in North India, merged into that movement; those churches are no longer considered Baptist. There are still court cases over the divided spoils (land, buildings, etc.) left behind by British Baptist missionaries.

Tradition says the Apostle Thomas sailed to India around AD 52. Many churches in the Karela State of South India, claim to be the result of Thomas's missionary work. My recount of non-Baptist Protestant churches is not based on research but on what I think I remember hearing while in India. I have included these rumors to give you a simplified and unofficial overview of denominations in India. *Now back to my main story.*

SAPIM filled a great missionary void, especially in the area of informal lay pastor training, evangelism, discipleship, and facilitating church planting. Baptists of many stripes sought our partnership while we sought some of those partnerships ourselves. When a Baptist group seemed to share common goals with us, and if there was mutual trust, we initiated temporary partnerships for lay pastor training. We also worked with several "baptistic" groups. Although they were not Baptist, they had similar beliefs and polity. Some of our partnerships were extended for other specified projects and goals. Some partnerships flourished while a few were short-lived. Subsidies tend to create dependency, so *SAPIM avoided using money for anything beyond training seminars.*

IMB (remember SAPIM was a very small part of IMB), used money to fund certain long-term projects like agriculture training, hospital work, and funding a professor at two theological colleges in India. *IMB also funded a few short-term projects* like radio programs, in order to saturate a target area with a gospel message; or disaster relief and hunger funds to alleviate human suffering. All projects run their course and end. *If outside money encourages local initiative, it can be very helpful. On the other hand, if outside money discourages local initiative, it leads to dependency, and that is very harmful and must be avoided.*

That is a universal truth about money. This is not the place to attempt a history with examples of both good and bad uses of subsidy by missionaries. We have all seen a similar dilemma in the use of money to help the poor and downtrodden in the USA. For example, "the war on poverty," one of many well-meaning government endeavors, has done as much harm as it has good.

Our collaborations enabled us to have the ear of Baptist leaders and enabled them to have our ear. It also enabled local Baptists and IMB to accomplish common goals together. The scripture says, "Iron sharpens iron." (Proverbs 27:17).

The result of most of those collaborations, of local Baptists and IMB missionary partners was an exciting church growth and discipleship in many parts of the region. Different methods in different areas led to good, yet differing results across those areas. *The agricultural work and lay pastor training efforts in the Orissa State of India that I was associated with produced the most successful, productive, and sustainable church growth.*

We also witnessed outstanding success working with OBEC (Orissa Baptist Evangelistic Crusade), a conglomeration of Baptist groups all across the state; *with Reverend. G. Samuel* and Baptist Church

Hyderabad, in Andra Pradesh; *with Rev. Nasir Masih*, in Chandigarh and across the North India States of Punjab, Haryana, Himachal Pradesh, and Jammu/Kashmir; *with Reverend Krupananda* and later, *with Pastor Vivian Fernandes* in Mumbai (Bombay) and Maharashtra State; *with Reverend. Divaker* and later, *with Reverend. A. Jacob* in Karnataka State; and *with Dr. Rebekah Naylor* of Bangalore Baptist Hospital.

All the leaders of our several primary work partner groups were worthy leaders and servants of God. However, Pastor Vivian Fernandes is characterized by all who know him: his congregation, his fellow pastors, and IMB missionaries, as the best example of a true "servant leader". He is one of the most humble men I know (humility finds strength in Christ, not in self; it is NOT weakness, nor self-depreciation). He is very unselfish, very teachable and God is working in and through Pastor Vivian to bring many to Christ and to grow and mature Christ's Church. We had many other smaller India collaborations with mixed results. Much good work was also being done in South Asia by non-SAPIM IMB missionaries in India, Pakistan, Nepal, Bangladesh, and Sri Lanka.

I must note two phenomenal people movements to Christ, of which I had no role or administrative oversight. The first, was in India among the Bhojpuri people. IMB missionaries D.W. and K.B. had some role in thousands and thousands coming to Christ. The second, was not in India, but still in South Asia. The number of new believers went from near zero to ten thousand, in a few short years and kept multiplying. This movement to Christ is among a very resistant mega-people group, sometimes referred to as "Cousins" by some. IMB missionary K.G. had some role in that. However, these types of movements to Christ, as well as what I witnessed in Orissa, India, are the work of God moving in and among local people.

Many Christians in "the West" seem enamored by secondhand experiences. We tend to delight in retelling another person's story yet often seem hesitant, even fearful, of telling our own story (the story of our own personal experience with the Living God).

An elaboration of IMB work in the state of Orissa, located on the central east coast of India, is in order. Orissa is one of the most economically impoverished states of India. Baptist work in Orissa began with British Baptist missionaries. Much later, Owen Cooper (mentioned earlier), began working with the Kui tribals of the Khond Hills and then handed that work over to IMB.

Under Dr. Clyde Meador's leadership, SALT (Sloping Agricultural Land Technology/Small Animal Land Technology/etc.) from the Philippines became successful in India as well.

Dr. S. N. Patra, professor of forestry at the State Agriculture University at Bhubaneswar, became a partner with IMB and helped coordinate our work among a coalition of Baptist groups in the Indian State of Orissa. Sometime around 1992-93, Dr. Meador sent Dr. Patra to the Philippines to train in SALT techniques at IMB's Rural Life Development Center in Mindanao. Dr. Patra became chairman of Asian Rural Life Development Foundation-India.

Sometime in 1993, John Langston (missionary journeyman) was sent to Orissa for two years to begin work on the newly purchased site for our *BOOST Center (Baptist Out of School Training)*. After finishing his two-year assignment, John returned to the USA. Calvin and Margaret Fox then moved from the Philippine project to continue and enlarge the Orissa agriculture ministries. It became a hub for training farmers, church planters, and lay pastors in various "off season food and cash crops," in "chronological Bible storying," and theologically through SAPIM seminars.

Since IMB work in Orissa fell under my general oversight, Dr. Patra helped me obtain a ten-year "business visa." In his letter of recommendation to the Indian government, Dr. Patra wrote (in part), "*Mr. Fred Beck* has been associated with Asian Rural Life Development Foundation and his expression of SALT and Bamboo techniques to farmers have been very useful, since his language of application is very layman.

"The Indian farmers are more comfortable and confident when a layman can teach them technologies using a nontechnological language they can understand."

"Mr. Beck's presence in different parts of the country will be a great help for food production among the rural poor. India is facing deforestation and environmental crisis. I am sure that SALT Technology and Bamboo propagation will bring fast changes in the hills, as well as plain agriculture in the waste lands." Signed, Dr. S. N. Patra

Dr. Patra and I worked well together—he the professional, I the nonprofessional. Although I was neither trained nor experienced in agriculture, I learned the SALT and bamboo propagation techniques and developed a troubleshooter's awareness of situations. The LORD also enabled me to explain technical agricultural truths in nontechnical language, through simple rural life illustrations, to uneducated rural farmers. We became a formidable team (the dynamic duo), even though duties throughout South Asia limited my time with Dr. Patra to visits of two weeks' duration, three or four times each year.

As mentioned earlier, besides training in sustainable agriculture, our training center, under the leadership of Calvin Fox, also taught lay pastors and laymen/laywomen how to tell adult Bible stories chronologically. Mr. Fox enlisted Rev. Sudhansu Naik (son-in-law of Brother Paul Prodhan) to help him teach the Bible stories and storying techniques. Meanwhile, Margaret Fox, Calvin's wife, made an impact on the local community by teaching spoken English and phonics in a local elementary school. She also taught reading and writing English to groups of local high school girls.

After a few years, Dr. Patra's brother, Dr. Biju Patra, who was in charge of communications for the state of Orissa, became the producer of a very successful set of Bible storying cassettes for Baptists. Bible stories were adapted to local folk music and were sung instead of being told. That was a somewhat common method of communication in rural areas of Orissa.

Those cassettes, as well as a weekly "Kui" language radio program on agriculture, medicine, and some gospel, were valuable tools used by laymen and laywomen (trained as "radio listener group leaders"). Those listener group leaders shared the Gospel and started new prayer groups in non-Christian villages. Great numbers of those radio listener groups led to thousands of conversions and hundreds of new churches.

The agricultural training addressed food and cash needs of the masses. Bible storying opened hearts to the Gospel. Calvin also hired an Indian medical doctor, Sanjeev Seelam, and his nurse-wife, Mammya, to work through his program. That produced astounding improvement in public health. Calvin raised funds to equip a vehicle for mobile health ministries and disaster response. Ours was a holistic approach to the people of Orissa. (See my memorial to Calvin, in Appendix C.)

I sometimes sent representative church planters, from different partners across India, to our agricultural project in Orissa. I wanted them to receive training in storying, basic agriculture, and public health. My goal was not for them to duplicate our work but to open their eyes to practical low-cost ways of meeting human need, for both basic food and health needs as well as for sharing the Gospel.

Because of our work with chronological Bible storying, I changed my preaching style to support and encourage that methodology. I could not do it chronologically because I was not in one place long enough. But as I was invited to preach across India, I storied the Bible then turned it into a discovery Bible study, asking questions about the story content. It was amazing that even when I storied through an interpreter, the local people were usually able to answer all my questions. They understood the stories, what God wanted them to know, and the implications for their own lives. I still use that method in the USA when I preach.

SAPIM continued to conduct at least fourteen weeklong lay pastor training seminars across Orissa each year. The number of lay pastors was growing rapidly because church growth was rapid.

One of my biggest disappointments in serving in South Asia was when I learned, about a year after departing South Asia for retirement, that one of our trusted local partners had shifted funds intended for an IMB project to his own personal ministry project. Even though I did not have responsibility for oversight of funds, I regret that I did not suspect or detect this sad situation.

Picture: Linda and I, with Brother and Mrs. Paul Prodhan.
*Bro. Paul was known as "the Apostle Paul" to his tribal people,
the Kui, of the Khond Hills, of the state of Orissa.*

Brother Paul's father, Poto Prodhan, was the first of the Kui tribe to follow Jesus. He died October 6, 1955 (age sixty-two) and was buried on land adjacent to the Mallikapuri Baptist Church building, built by British Baptist missionaries.

The Kui tribal people practiced human sacrifice as late as the mid-1950s. Children were used in those sacrifices. I was told that the last human sacrifice was done less than two hundred yards from the Mallikapuri church, but that no members participated.

Paul made his living selling tea leaves throughout the Khond Hills. On his deathbed, Poto called his son to him and said, "Paul, you must evangelize our people." Paul responded by saying he did not have training to do that. But his dad insisted, saying, "The missionaries have all gone from our hills, there is no one else to go.

Besides, why do you think I named you Paul. You must now become 'the Apostle Paul' to our people."

"Pastor Paul stories" are unending. Each telling examples of how that simple humble man-and-wife team suffered beatings and other hardships while walking through (then) Bengal tiger–infested forests (often sleeping outdoors), taking the Gospel to their people, and bringing them to Christ.

Earlier, I used the term "the impossible lifestyle" of the SAPIM missionaries (living out of our suitcase for up to four months at a time for a total of at least eight months each year). During our first semester in India, we slept in nearly a hundred different beds, but decided we need not count beds. *During that first semester, I also realized that the more we served "the least of these," the fewer complaints we had about our austere lifestyle. I was also more content and fulfilled than ever before.*

The bi-vocational lay pastors (farmers, laborers, teachers, etc.) we trained were very appreciative and grew in their personal relationship with the Lord. They used their training to make necessary adjustments in their own ministries. As a result, their churches grew and multiplied. With all that happening, we were blessed beyond measure.

Therefore I no longer considered mine to be "an impossible lifestyle." So when, on occasion, we drew an unclean hotel and I needed to run to a shop to buy a bottle of cleanser/disinfectant and a brush to clean the bathroom and toilet before it could be used, it became a minor inconvenience instead of ruining my day. *It was a matter of perspective, and God was changing mine.*

Scripture tells us, "I/we can do all things through Christ, who strengthens me/us" (Philippians 4:13). Why then should we be amazed when biblical truth becomes self-evident and apropos? Instead of amazement, we should "thank Christ Jesus our Lord, who strengthened me/us, because He considered me/us faithful, putting me/us into service; even though I/we was/were formerly ..." (1 Timothy 1:12).

Ephesians 4:11–12 is my favorite scripture describing the role/task of ministers of the gospel, which is "the equipping of the saints" (all believers) for the work of ministry/service, to the building up of the body of Christ (the Church). Thus the ministry belongs to all believers, not just the ordained ministers. Then Ephesians 4:13–16 discloses what will happen when all the saints carry out their ministries; mature believers, who are no longer deceived, but rather speak the truth in love and grow in Christlikeness. That, in turn, enables all believers to live in harmony, exercising their individual gifts, producing growth of the entire body (the Church) in love.

First Peter 5:1–7 reveals some other responsibilities of Christian ministers. In Verse one, Peter says, "I exhort the *elders* among you as your fellow elder in…" Verse two adds, "*Shepherd* the flock of God among you…" and Verse 2 also adds, "*exercising oversight…*". I believe Peter is explaining the three main roles of the pastor. (1) The Greek word "presbuteros" (*elder*) recognizes the spiritual maturity (an example) of a true pastor (Acts 14:23, 15:22, 20:17, First Timothy 5:17, Titus 1:5), (2) "poimen" (*shepherd*) is a true pastor who tends, feeds, protects, and leads his flock (Acts 20:28, Ephesians 4:11), and (3) "episkopos" (*bishop/overseer*) a true pastor has stewardship responsibility of the local congregation (Acts 20:28, Philippians 1:1, First Timothy 3:2, Titus 1:7). Thus, the will of God, not the pastor's will, is the true pastor's purpose (First Peter 5:1), leading with humility (5:3) is his style of leadership and being a model for his congregation to follow (5:3) is his "modes operandi", all done as an under-shepherd to our Lord, the Chief Shepherd (5:4).

Another way to express that is "discipleship," which begins with pre-evangelism, then evangelism and continues in the process of spiritual maturity or Christlikeness of individual believers and the Church itself.

Jesus's statement of that is in the "Great Commission" in Matthew 28:18–20. "All authority has been given to Me in heaven and on earth. Go therefore and make disciples of all the nations (every ethnic group), baptizing them in the name of the Father and the Son and the Holy Spirit, teaching them to observe all that I commanded you; and lo, I am with you always, even to the end of the age" (NASV).

I often teach that "discipleship" is "four ones and three twos" (1 Corinthians 11:1 and 2 Timothy 2:2). It's an oversimplification, but addresses the heart of the matter. We, who serve, must encourage the people we disciple in matters of faith and ministry to "be imitators of me, just as I also am of Christ" (1 Corinthians 11:1). "The things which you have heard from me in the presence of many witnesses, these entrust to faithful men, who will be able to teach others also" (2 Timothy 2:2).

Therefore our service or ministry is not primarily teaching people what to do but rather becoming a living demonstration or embodiment of what it means to follow Jesus every day, in every situation and relationship that life brings our way. In reality, this pattern is not only for Christian leaders, it is for every believer. In that matter, God is not yet finished with me.

Two simple personal illustrations of imitating/modeling Christ: Years before, in Tegal, Indonesia, I visited a couple, to whom I had been witnessing. The wife was a new believer, but her husband resisted the gospel. One day, I rode my Vespa scooter to their *kampung* (edge of city village) a half mile from our house. When I left their house, the Vespa would not start. Young boys had put dirt into my fuel tank. After learning the problem, I pushed the Vespa home, without anger or complaint. The following week, the man and his wife showed up at our weekly Bible study. Pak (Mr.) Rodjikin told me that my teaching had not interested Him, but when he saw me demonstrating the teaching and attitude of Christ, after my Vespa had been disabled by kids in his village, he *"wanted to know more about Fred's Jesus."*

A few years later, while assigned to Klaten, Indonesia, I rode the Vespa to a village where I was assisting a city church start a new rural congregation. One day, en route to the village, I had a flat tire but was able to put on the spare tire and continue on. Several years later, while we served in Ambon, fellow missionaries Bill and Liz Corwin called me from Jakarta. They told me of a young pastor who claimed that I had been very influential in him becoming a believer.

They told me his name, but I did not know who he was. They continued, saying he told the church that Fred Beck talked with him while changing the tire on his Vespa, and that conservation later led to his faith in Christ and now he was a pastor. *I remember changing the flat tire; I don't remember talking to that young man. We are often more successful when we naturally respond to people in unplanned situations than we are in our planned witnessing encounters.*

Thus, in India, I was often reminded of that which I had learned earlier in Indonesia. *God sent me overseas, not for what I could do for Him but so He could do in me, that which He desires.* It is only as we allow the Lord free rein to accomplish His purpose in us is He able to accomplish, through us, that which He desires. We cannot do God's work for Him. God's work is God-sized, and we are not God. In John 15:5, Jesus said, "Apart from Me, you can do nothing." *Only God can do God's work.*

Is that a lazy man's out? No! It is simply learning to live in total dependency on God. That is not easy, and I'm not there yet, but neither am I where I used to be. All believers have God's promise that, "He will complete the good work He began in us" (Philippians 1:6). The indwelling Holy Spirit is God's down payment and God's evidence that we already belong to Him (Ephesians 1:3–4).

Even though God chooses to use people to do His bidding, it is evident that God does not need us. He is able to accomplish His plans without us. I will share three, of many, examples of God working through dreams and visions of Jesus.

Nelama's son was in the Bangalore Baptist Hospital with an illness that doctors in her town could not treat. Nelama (not her real name) was not a believer, but she entered the hospital chapel to pray for her son. There she had a vision of a bearded doctor who went in and touched her son. After seeing the vision, she rushed to her son's room and discovered her son was healed—completely recovered. Nelama interpreted the vision as a visit from the "Great Physician." The following week, BBH held a routine "seekers' conference"; *Nelama attended* with three friends. She testified of Jesus, and eight ladies responded to Christ.

There was an older Bangladeshi man who had fought for independence (against West Pakistan) in 1971. He was called Freedom Fighter by missionaries, protecting his identity. He had come to Jesus through a vision of Jesus. He lived in a place where following Jesus could mean death. "Freedom Fighter" became a very bold witness. He said, "I was ready to die for my country in 1971. Now, I am ready to die for my Savior." *This man led over a hundred men to Christ, in the first half of 2001.*

Orissa, India*: Santosh (not his real name) was not a believer. He and his Hindu friends, from a rural area, were put in jail because they injured several town people in a street brawl.* A Baptist pastor went to that jail to preach Christ. That night, *Jesus appeared to Santosh in a dream.* Jesus told him that he would be released from jail in three days. Three days later, he and his friends were released. Santosh hurried home to his village to tell his father about the Baptist preacher and that Jesus has spoken to him in a dream. Everything Jesus told him in the dream came true. Santosh's father sent requests that several Baptist pastors be sent to preach to them. *Six months later, over 1,200 had been baptized.*

Jesus appearing in dreams and visions is God taking the initiative to make himself known to "people who have no witness." Many who receive God's direct witness become believers. Abraham (Genesis 12:1) is a biblical example of that. Also Joshua 24:1-3.

I have learned I need not compare myself to any other person. *We are simply commanded to be faithful stewards with whatever the Lord has entrusted to us: be it relationships, spiritual gifts, talents, skills, ministries, money, etc.* Success in life is determined by obedience to God, not by the world's standards, evaluations, or judgments about success.

For several summers, after transferring to SAPIM, we were loaned back to Indonesia because India churches had busy summer schedules and didn't have time for our training then. During those summer assignments in Indonesia, we might cover for a furloughing missionary or be assigned special projects that the Indonesian Mission was unable to fulfill due to personnel restraints (i.e., home follow-ups of released patients of one of the Baptist hospitals). It also enabled Matt, our then teenage youngest son, to be among old friends and attend summer camp with them.

One of those occasions, around 1992, I taught "Romans" in a "J term" at the Baptist seminary in Semarang. During that time, Ken Ellison (fellow missionary) arranged for us to visit Tegal and its rural areas one weekend. When we moved from Java to Ambon in 1985, I had given my address book of people I had worked with throughout our nine years in Tegal to Ken. So Ken contacted one church to host us for a weekend. Unexpectedly, we were blessed to visit old friends and churches that we served during our first assignment in Tegal, Central Java, 1971–1980.

One village congregation, a half hour east of Tegal, invited me to preach (in Indonesian of course). It was very special for Linda, Matt, and I, because they also invited many Christian families from scattered villages across that vast area. Those were people whom I had led to Christ, then grounded in the Scriptures, twelve years earlier. After worship, we ate together and talked of old and new times with those dear friends whom we had not seen since we moved from Tegal to Klaten in 1980.

It was God's affirmation for our years of struggle to get the gospel to people living in an anti-Christian environment. More than that, it affirmed the power of God's word planted in the hearts of new believers who remained faithful to God, even though they had no trained leaders to continue teaching them.

To top it off, members of our host church told me that the village where I had the Bible study, which stopped after radical Muslims frightened the people (pages 83-84) has a Baptist church. *Those men, whom I taught for only a few weeks, later went to Jakarta for work. They came to Christ in Jakarta. When they returned to their village, they brought the Gospel with them. Now you know the rest of that story. What had appeared to be a victory for Satan was reversed by the powerful love and mercy of God into victory to His glory.* Trust God and leave results to Him.

I had not wanted to serve in India. I, like many other people, assumed I knew what was best for me and my family. There was no place for India, in my equation. However, "our" knowledge is limited and "our" perspective is based on an incomplete conception of reality. God's plan for each of us is not only about us; it is much larger, encompassing eternity, as well as the present.

Speaking through the Prophet Jeremiah (29:11), God says, "I know the plans I have for you, plans for welfare and not for calamity to give you a future and a hope." That promise of God was given through Jeremiah, even as God was sending the people of Judah into seventy years of captivity in Babylon. That was punishment for their idolatry. When Judah returned to their own land seventy years later, they no longer worshiped idols. God continued to bless and protect Judah during captivity in Babylon; then after Judah's return from captivity, God continued His good plans to give the promised Savior to mankind through Judah.

Jesus said, "I came that they may have life and have it abundantly" (John 10:10).

I shudder at the thought that my former prejudice against India nearly caused me to skip God's best for me. Had I not obeyed God and gone to India, I would have missed the most fulfilling and productive years of my overseas ministry. God is patient with us. He is also full of love and grace for us.

My prayer, for you, who read my testimony, is that you will not reject God's plans for your life and witness. God's plan for each of us results in the very best, the most meaningful, and satisfying life possible. Please do not miss it. However our own fulfillment is not the goal for believers, it is a by-product of seeking God and following His plans for us. The life of faith is God-centered, not self centered. We seek to please God, not ourselves.

Retirement and Beyond

uring our 1998 furlough in Amarillo, I asked God if it was
okay to plan to retire in 2002, after completing one more
term overseas. So I, like many others, tried to explain to
God that which He already knew. I told Him that we were growing
weary after years of itinerant work, in what might be described by
some as difficult places. We would be even more weary after our
next four years. I told Him that family is important to us, and I
wanted Linda to be able to spend some healthy years visiting our
adult children and our grandchildren. I had growing concerns for
Linda's health; she had high blood pressure, etc. I did not blame it
all on her. I admitted to God that I wanted to retire as well. There
was also another reason; I have seen some Christian leaders stay in
their position too long. I felt that I was doing a reasonably good job,
however situations were changing, new opportunities were opening.

It would be an ideal time for a change of leadership. One with fresh ideas, a different set of gifts and personal strengths who could, by God's grace, take the work to higher levels.

My children did not believe that I would retire then, not sure Linda did either. While on business in Richmond, Virginia, I shared my thoughts with Avery and Shirley Willis, dear friends, former peers in Indonesia, who then served as vice president of IMB. Upon arriving back in Asia, I shared the same with my boss, Clyde Meador. I continued to talk to the Lord about this, and although He never gave me a clear answer, He did give me peace about it. Subsequent events and personal ministries involvement since our retirement have, in my mind, confirmed my opinion that it was time for my retirement. And of course, the work in South Asia has continued to expand and thrive without me and others.

In January 2001, Linda and I began making final trips to places and people across vast areas of South Asia, the subcontinent (India, Pakistan, Bangladesh, Nepal, Bhutan, Sri Lanka, and the Maldives). *How do you leave so many people and places where you have seen God's grace and His life-giving, life-changing miracles at work?* Good-byes are never easy, especially when those good-byes are for the rest of your lifetime on earth. However, our good-byes were a mixture of sadness and joy. Tears, yes, but great joy because of shared lives, shared ministries, and abundance of results that will last into and throughout eternity.

We received many letters, certificates, and memory gifts from people we cannot forget. Those gifts now decorate our home and spur us to rejoice in our past, even as we live in our new present.

One such gracious recognition is from the Baptists of Orissa.

Rev. Fred Beck & Mrs. Linda Beck
"We discover in both of you the blessing & joys of developing a
Growing relationship with God, family and the self
In the tireless service that both have been sharing for His glory.

God works through you to achieve His purposes, it is grace on His
part. Hence there is delight, joy and wonder
as He works through you and we witness and respond
with gratitude & humility for worthy disciples of Christ.

God enables you to communicate truth in special, powerful ways.
His gift of Wisdom helps guiding others toward goodness of Life.

God speaks to us through your great contributions
to the Baptists of Orissa and for His Church.

Today, the May 6th 2001 at the United Theological School in
Cuttack, we humbly recognize your
Life full of challenges for His mission & pray to our mighty God to
Protect you both for His purpose as we prayerfully encourage
To press on ... with renewed strength ... like the eagle."

signed	signed
Rev. H C Nanda	Shri Susil Kumar Sahu
Principal	President
United Theological School, Cuttack	All Orissa Baptist Churches
	Foundation

We received several oil paintings and a large charcoal portrait of
Linda and me surrounded by faces of people we had served. Those are
all hanging on our walls. *One of my favorite gifts, was from an Indian
friend. It is an 8x10 picture he took of me* sitting on the ground under a
straw roof shelter. I was with a group of poor farmers. Superimposed,
on a corner of the picture are the words, *"Rev. Fred Beck, friend of the
friendless."* Very few people have seen that picture. Most will never
see it. It is not framed hanging on my wall. It is in a folder in my file
cabinet. I must admit it tempts "my pride," yet is a favorite anyway.
It causes me to pray that, one day, I will be able to personify that com-
pliment (friend of the friendless) from a dear friend.

Thus with mixed emotions, we departed Asia the latter part of August 2001. We had built up a lot of leave time, so our final "Stateside assignment/furlough" would last fourteen months. Our actual retirement date would be the first day of October 2002. *I would then be sixty-four, eleven months short of sixty-five and Linda would be sixty-two. We had served overseas for thirty-three years and five months.* Prior to that, we had served as pastor of three churches; two of which were bi-vocational pastorates (Energy, Texas, and Esparto, California), the third as full-time pastor of FBC, Folsom, California.

Our transition back to the USA full-time was made relatively easy because we had spent our last five six-month furloughs in Amarillo, as members of First Baptist Church. Our daughter, Pam, and family, as well as many established friendships from earlier furloughs are here; thus we felt at home. We purchased our first home in January 2002, nine months before retirement. By God's grace, our mortgage was paid off in early 2015.

We were active and faithful to our church but did not take on any leadership roles for a few years. We (especially me) were both involved in promoting overseas missions through speaking engagements and many weeklong conferences, called "On Mission Celebrations," in Baptist churches all across the USA.

Linda suffered a heart attack and triple bypass surgery in February 2005. We completed our conference commitments that year, with the exception of one in Galveston, Texas. We had to cancel our involvement there because Linda needed more recuperation. Sadly, we missed the only opportunity we ever had to return to our "home-town," to speak. We took no more IMB assignments after 2005, although we occasionally have opportunity to share in churches closer to home.

Linda's health improved, and she began to take on more roles at FBC. She had already become deeply involved in WMU and adult ESL. Now she began to accept church committee assignments and teaching adult Sunday school. She also accepted several adult literacy students, one at a time, but no longer has a literacy student. She had taught many Indonesians to read and write their own language years before. She had even taught one group of Javanese women to read and write their language, even though Linda did not speak Javanese herself.

For many years, Linda and I served as "election officials." After a few years, Linda was appointed as an "election judge" and served in that capacity four or five years. We both retired from that work in 2015.

I was slower to get into the harness at FBC. I had served in the forefront overseas for many years. Now, I want to serve in nonspotlight ministries. I received training in *adult literacy* and have had several students, the last three of whom have been Muslims from Kuwait, the Sudan, and now Afghanistan. I seek to serve them in hopes that they will be able to read and write English correctly and improve their salary opportunities. I also pray they will choose to follow my Lord. I bear witness, but only God's Spirit can give them faith through the word of God.

I teach *Bible stories chronologically* to adult ESL students during an assembly time. I plant the Word in their head, and ESL teachers are faithful to give a personal witness throughout the eight-month ESL year. The Holy Spirit has moved the truth from the heads to the hearts of many students and birthed faith in Christ.

Our church is involved in *Texas Baptist Disaster Relief* across the USA. We have a shower and laundry trailer with six individual showers, two washing machines, and two dryers. Our team of volunteers takes the trailer to disaster areas when called out by disaster officials. We minister for as long as needed. Our motto is, "Anyway. Anytime. Anywhere." We also serve as a support team for many mission opportunities in Amarillo and mission trips in places without showers/laundry, for those on mission. *I was privileged to serve as director of that work for three years.* I still serve, as one of the leaders, for now.

God willing, I will soon start my seventh year of volunteer involvement in *Christian Men and Women's Job Corps.* I have served as mentor, teacher, and "general flunky" in that fruitful high-witness ministry. Participants from the Amarillo community as well as incarcerated men and women tend to be very responsive and appreciative. For sixteen weeks, each semester, we help our adult participants improve their work ethic, develop a career plan, and teach them essential soft skills needed to get and hold a job. Our graduates usually get jobs. Our program has been adopted into the *Randall County Jail's "PREP Program."* PREP prepares men and women to be able to make it after their release from prison, and most PREP graduates do not return to prison.

I have also had the joy of *teaching the Bible to fifteen to twenty older adult men, in a Sunday school class, for the past seven years.*

Some may *say I have "too many irons in the fire." However, I would quickly respond, "I'm just happy to have a fire, in which to place my irons."*

Linda and I do not serve others to gain salvation or reward, nor do I mention those volunteer ministries to impress anyone. Many people invested their lives in us and others. We too enjoy investing in the lives of people. We serve in obedience to our LORD. We seek to demonstrate His love to others and glorify Him, in the eyes of all. *That is part of our worship to God.*

Ephesians 2:8–10 makes it clear that it is only "by grace you have been saved through faith; and that not of yourselves, it is the gift of God; not as a result of works, that no one should boast. For we are His workmanship, created in Christ Jesus for good works, which God prepared beforehand, that we should walk in them" (NASV).

Missions (bearing witness to the saving grace of God through Christ to people in Jerusalem, Judea, Samaria, and the uttermost parts of the earth) and lovingly serving others are major ingredients in the life of a "follower of Christ." However, our first obligation and the most essential element of a believer's life is to worship God alone and to obey, enjoy and glorify Him.

Sometimes, scripture and poems, set to music, best speak of the worship intent of our heart. I mention only a few of the thousands of examples:

Higher Calling
LeBlanc

Down at Your feet, oh Lord, is the most high place;
in Your presence, Lord, I seek Your face.
There is no higher calling, no greater honor
than to bow and kneel before Your throne.
I'm amazed at Your glory, embraced by Your mercy.
Oh Lord, I live to worship You.

Here I Am to Worship
Hughes
Here I am to worship, here I am to bow down,
Here I am to say that You're my God.
You're altogether lovely, altogether worthy,
Altogether wonderful to me.

The Bible
Psalm 42:1

As the deer pants for water,
So my soul pants for you, O God.

The Bible
Psalm 100:1

Shout joyfully to the LORD, all the earth.
Serve the LORD with gladness;
Come before Him with joyful singing.
Know that the LORD Himself is God;
It is He who has made us, and not we ourselves;
We are the sheep of His pasture.
Enter His gates with thanksgiving

And His courts with praise.
Give thanks to Him, bless His name.
For the LORD is good;
His lovingkindness is everlasting
And His faithfulness to all generations.

Thus I conclude these vignettes of my life, even as I began, basking in God's multifaceted grace, which includes love, joy, peace, mercy, forgiveness, renewal, worth, hope, security, etc.

Praise the One True and Living God of Abraham.

AMEN

Prissy (L) and Lady (R), our retirement foster children Small female house
dogs have most always been a part of my life.
(Princess, Tippy, Frisky, Boneka [Doll], Prissy, and Lady)

Following page: Retirement family photo (2002). Since then,
we have added two more grandsons and five great-grandsons. We
expect more to come, including some great-granddaughters. Our
first granddaughter, not pictured, is already in the presence of God.

Epilogue

I was a wounded person during my childhood and early youth. I was neither victimized by unloving parents nor by some abusive person. My wounds were all self-inflicted—the result of selfishness and poor choices, as well as, twisted thinking and behavior. *It was what the Bible calls "sin" and "the wages of sin is always death," including "spiritual death."*

At age fifteen, I hit bottom and came to the end of self. I reached out to God and His grace. A chorus, by Coltrell, describes what transpired when I cried out to God:

> I come broken to be mended; I come wounded to be healed.
> I come desperate to be rescued, I come empty to be filled.
> I come guilty to be pardoned by the blood of Christ the Lamb.
> And I'm welcomed with open arms, praise God, just as I am.

Yes, welcomed by God, just as I was. But praise God, true to His promise, He did not leave me in that condition. God gave me new life and repurposed me—what the Bible describes as being "born again spiritually," alive to a present and eternal personal relationship with the One True Living God, the God of Abraham.

I also acknowledge that these "autobiographical vignettes" are, as the meaning of the phrase implies, *selected vignettes*, not a complete biography. I also included only a small portion of our thirty-three-plus years of overseas experiences. My purpose was to share only a few of those experiences as representative of the whole and to indicate how my missionary experience was God's tool to change me. He changed me so He could use me as a tool to help proclaim His grace to humanity, help disciple new followers of Christ, help build and mature His church (the Body of Christ), and to help train and equip a biblically based spiritual leadership for His church.

It is my prayer, that you, the reader of my simple tome, worship the One True Living God and enjoy a daily personal relationship with Him. If so, you too have experienced His grace. Please share His grace with others by your attitude, actions, and words through normal everyday relationships, as well as through intentional relationships outside your comfort zone.

May you, by God's grace, also become a vehicle in sharing and demonstrating the story of the "biblical worldview," that although "all (mankind) have sinned and fallen short of the glory of God (God's purpose for us), God is in the process of creating a new race of humanity."

From a humanity fallen and flawed by willful personal and corporate sin, God is creating a new humanity. Thus the sinner who repents of his rebellion against God and by faith accepts and obeys God's gracious provision, for eternal salvation in Christ is adopted into God's family and His eternal plan for mankind.

God takes penitent sinners and begins a lifelong process of transforming "a worm into a butterfly." God has begun recreating penitent rebels. They are *not* renewed in the image of an innocent first Adam, susceptible to sin.

Instead God is recreating penitent humanity into the image of the second Adam. The second Adam is Jesus the Christ. In the birth of Jesus, the eternal God, Creator, and Sustainer became man also.

Jesus did not sin, not even once. He was tempted as are we, yet He did not sin. Jesus came to earth not as a great teacher and example, but as the Sinless Lamb of God—God's provision for our sin. We need only accept God's provision of grace and yield ourselves in obedience to Him. The believer is no longer a rebel against God, but rather a forgiven sinner, whose sins have been paid for by the crucified and resurrected Savior. He conquered death, the penalty for sin, for us, that we may have eternal life in Him.

Having justified the sinner by grace through faith, God begins the task of changing the nature of the justified sinner. He transforms us, from an Adam likeness, into Christlikeness. God changes the saved sinner from having an inclination to sin into a new creation, with an inclination to not sin. This new mankind loves, obeys, and worships God alone. This work of grace is done by the indwelling Spirit of God. This change is not completed until God comes to receive us unto Himself.

That metamorphosis does not take place in a cocoon, but within the crucible of a believer's daily life on this earth. It is God at work in the life and heart of the person of faith. That work of God continues even into the process of death, until the believer draws his or her last breath. This lifelong process is often referred to as *sanctification.*

Sanctification can be compared to an inverted roller-coaster ride. In a roller-coaster ride, the passenger is carried up to the highest point on the ride and then released to the laws of gravity, in a ride consisting of a series of ups and downs, with a generally downward trajectory, ending where the ride first began.

However, in God's work of the sanctification of the believer, the believer begins where he is. Then he/she is empowered by God's indwelling Spirit through ups and downs. However, the general trajectory of those ups and downs are upward, not downward. Thus in this work of God, believers do not end up where they began but rather end up where they have never been before.

That brings believers to *glorification,* the final earthly stage of God's work of grace, in all who believe. That means that the grace of God has completely transformed the believer, and he or she is now ready to stand in the very presence of God, forever glorifying God and enjoying an everlasting life unimaginable to our present finite minds.

So, in short, the "biblical worldview" is that God is in the process of creating a new humanity in the likeness of the Resurrected Jesus. A new humanity which can, by God's grace, resist sin and is fit to dwell with the God of Abraham, the One True and Living God forever (a concept introduced to me by Dr. Nat Tracy at Howard Payne College, in 1958, as the "Christian worldview").

Therefore the "Good News of God" we are called to is not a life of "do nots." It is a call to an abundant life in Christ. A life of unlimited challenge and opportunity. It is a life of learning to forgive and enable others, even as we have been forgiven and enabled by God and others. It is also a life of learning to enjoy giving more than receiving, yet becoming humble and gracious enough to allow others to help and bless us. All that and more are the challenges and joys of following Jesus.

Before concluding this volume, allow this "has been" missionary to share an oversimplified version of what missions means, as well as share an oversimplified history of Christian missions.

"Missions: God's Heartbeat" was the title of the sermon I preached when God got my personal attention about joining Him in His missionary enterprise to all nations (*panta ta ethne*, literally "to every ethnicity/every people group").

Some people seem to think that the world is like a pancake, thus they often view missions as pouring syrup on a pancake. Just get the gospel out there and everyone will have a fair chance.

However, a missionary sees the world not as a pancake, but rather more like a Belgian waffle. You don't just pour syrup on a waffle. The syrup does not naturally flow from one walled-off socket to the neighboring sockets. To get the syrup into every socket, one must intentionally pour syrup into each individual socket. That is a different ball game.

Both the Old Testament and the New Testament seek to tell us that. God's love for the nations and God's plan for the salvation of all nations refers to every ethnic group/people group/affinity group within every nation. God's love for all nations/peoples is one of the themes of the entire Bible. People is a plural word, but in God's plan, "peoples" is correct. An ethnic group is made up of many people (plural). Since God loves every ethnic group, all those ethnic groups become the peoples of earth, thus *peoples* refers to a plurality of plurals.

Some seem to think that only minority groups are ethnics. That is incorrect; we are all ethnics. Therefore, in reality, *missions* is a cross-cultural endeavor. Like getting syrup into a different socket of the waffle—one that beforehand had no syrup. The most successful missions' endeavors often/usually involve communicating the gospel through another language, the language of those being reached.

Once an ethnic group has a critical mass of strong indigenous churches, led by indigenous people, they can continue to evangelize their own people without outside help. Those churches should also become missionary churches and reach out to other ethnic groups, which have not yet received syrup in their socket within the waffle.

The history of missions begins with God's creation of the universe. It picks up clarification with the call of Abraham and God's choice of an unlikely people group, the Hebrews, to become the avenue through whom God makes Himself known to the world. It was also through the Hebrews that God Himself would become man also. God's plan was to save mankind from our sin and create a new humanity in the pattern of a resurrected Jesus,

Christian missions picked up speed with two events. *First* was the death and resurrection of Jesus and Him giving the great commission to a group of ragtag followers, just prior to His ascension to heaven. The *second* is the ascension of Jesus and the coming of God's Spirit upon each individual believer, beginning ten days after Jesus's ascension, on the Day of Pentecost.

The missions movement followed the pattern of the Great Commission, restated on the day Jesus ascended, "You will receive power when the Holy Spirit has come upon you; and you shall become My witnesses both in Jerusalem, Judea, and Samaria, and even to the remotest part of the earth" (Acts 1:8).

Thus the Gospel spread from Jerusalem, Judea, and Samaria to Ethiopia in North Africa then Syria, Cyprus, and Asia Minor and Turkey. After that, it jumped to Southern Europe to Macedonia, Greece, Italy, and slowly progressed throughout Europe. From Europe to India, central and lower Africa. From Europe, the Gospel also jumped across the Atlantic Ocean to South, Central, and North America.

From the New World, it jumped the Pacific Ocean and began to spread through China and the rest of Asia, Today, the Gospel is spreading in Central Asia and the Middle East. We anticipate the Gospel will soon spread throughout the Middle East, North Africa, and to Israel, coming full circuit back to where it first began. The force of missions has always been God's Spirit and a maturing mission field, which then becomes a new missions force.

Some feel that when the Gospel returns to Israel, Christ will return. Perhaps, however, in referring to the end of time, Jesus tells us, "It is not for you to know times or epochs which the Father has fixed by His own authority" (Acts 1:7). And continued by saying we are to be His witnesses unto all the earth, as quoted earlier (Acts 1:8). Even so, come, Lord Jesus, Maranatha!

Grace, love, joy and peace to you, in the Lord.

Appendix A

Divine and Angelic Encounters, Interventions, and Interactions with Mankind

Again and again, the Bible gives clear evidence that God speaks to mankind and acts in their behalf. For example:

Genesis 12:1: "Now the LORD said to Abram, 'Go forth from your country, and from your relatives and from your father's house, to the land which I will show you.'"

Genesis 45:4–5 "Joseph said to his brothers, 'I am your brother Joseph, whom you sold into Egypt. Now do not be grieved or angry with yourselves, because you sold me here, for God sent me before you to preserve life.'"

Second Corinthians 12:2 and 4, the Apostle Paul said, "I know a man in Christ who fourteen years ago ... was caught up into Paradise, and heard inexpressible words, which a man is not permitted to speak."

About angels, Hebrews 1:14 says, "Are they not ministering spirits, sent out (by God) to render service for the sake of those who will inherit salvation?"

Hebrews 13:2 says, "Do not neglect to show hospitality to strangers, for some have entertained angles without knowing it." (for an example of this read Genesis 18:1 f).

Although I rarely talk about it, Linda and/or I have experienced encounters with God and at least once encountered an angel. We have also witnessed God's intervention to lead us to His will and to also spare us and others tragedy. *Actually, I have already mentioned several such events in earlier pages.*

I will share a few of many other such events with you even though in so doing, some may accuse me of going off the deep end. I take that risk in order to bear witness to God's power and glory as well as His love and protection of His people, according to His own will and plan.

I am not implying that I am an extra special person or that God provided experiences for me that He does not provide for others. Many people have given witness of similar encounters. Many others, including unbelievers (Muslims and Hindus), have experienced dreams or visions of Jesus Himself; I have not.

First: In 1979, Linda, Matt, and I were driving home to Tegal (Central Java, Indonesia). Darkness overtook us just prior to entering the outskirts of our city. The narrow road, flanked by poorly lit homes and small shops, was filled with headlights from both directions.

Suddenly, from the extremity of my side vision, *a small child darted in front of an automobile approaching from the other direction. I was certain that child would be hit by that car. I yelled out, "JESUS! Help!"* There was not time to even complete my plea. Unbelievably, the boy escaped from being crushed by that car, but now he was a few feet in front of me.

There was no way for me to miss him. We were so close; he disappeared from my view. I thought I felt a slight bump on the left side of my bumper. I stopped as soon as possible and got out of the car.

The Indonesian police warn drivers to never stop after an accident but drive to the nearest police station and turn yourself in. Otherwise, you risk being beaten to death. I could not do that. I had to stop and try to help that child. A small crowd had gathered instantly, but much to my amazement, the child was unhurt and safe in the arms of his Muslim parents. They were gracious and told me, "Tidak apa apa" (It's nothing, meaning he's okay, go on).

We departed quickly, praising God for sparing that child. That night, although we did not see them, we encountered God or one of His angels. Later, at home and settled down, I realized that God had not only spared the child, He spared Linda, Matt, and I as well.

Second: In the fall of 1990, we were traveling in the Indian State of Orissa, with Jim and Carolyn McAtee. There was a typhoon off the coast, and we were traveling away from the coast, in two rented taxies. We were attempting to reach Malikapuri, to conduct a five-day training conference for bi-vocational pastors. Torrential rains slowed our progress.

Suddenly, a village farmer appeared in the road ahead, waving a storm lantern. The Sikh drivers stomped the brakes and managed to stop the vehicles. Jim and I, along with the drivers, got out of the vehicles into the rain. We walked ahead to the top of a slight rise in the highway and discovered the bridgeless low water crossing was covered by a storm-flooded torrent of raging water. We learned later that a busload of passengers had been swept to their death from that crossing prior to our arrival.

We walked around looking for the farmer who had flagged us down and probably saved our lives. We wanted to thank him. However, there was no one there. We are confident that we had seen an angel who appeared to us as a farmer.

Third: In 1971, not long after finishing language school and moving to our first assignment in Tegal (Central Java). Linda and I, accompanied by our three children (Matt had not yet been born), were driving to the city of Semarang, where the Baptist seminary was located. We left home late Sunday afternoon and stopped in the town of Pekalongan to worship in one of our struggling churches. Pekalongan is located an hour east of Tegal.

After evening services, we piled back into the Volkswagen mini-bus and continued the three-hour journey to Semarang. This was not our first trip to Pekalongan. It was, however, our first trip beyond Pekalongan; thus the highway was new to me.

About an hour beyond Pekalongan, the narrow highway became very curvy. We became trapped behind a slow-moving truck, for several miles. Darkness had set in, and it began to rain very lightly. Finally, the highway took a long wide right curve, and I could see a straight road ahead. There were no headlights approaching, so I gained speed and passed the slow-moving truck. We found ourselves in a dense teak forest. The road was straight ahead, as far as I could see; however the headlights on our old minibus did not reach too far ahead.

Suddenly a huge lightning bolt lit up the road ahead and I realized a sharp curve was fast approaching. I soon discovered that the curve was actually a hairpin curve. Somehow, I was able to negotiate that dangerous curve on a rain-slick highway and not crash into the teak forest. An hour later, we arrived safely in Semarang.

That lightning strike was the only lightning we saw that night. The rain was very light, not a storm. The lightning lit up the danger we faced at the most strategic time. Was all that just a coincidence? Maybe, but in my opinion, it was an act of God. What some call a coincidence is often God acting incognito.

Fourth: In early 1975, Linda was pregnant with our fourth child. We were living in Purwokerto, Central Java (in the home of Von and Marge Worten, who were on furlough), while we updated a recently purchased house in Tegal. A house that had no indoor kitchen or bathroom, only one bedroom, no running water, and with little electricity. We also taught seminary extension classes, filling in for the Wortens; even as I traveled back and forth to Tegal, a four-hour round-trip, to oversee work on our mission house.

There was a development project an hour away from Purwokerto, and several older American engineers and their wives lived on site. They invited Linda and me to drive over once a week to have a meal with them and lead them in Bible study. Teaching in English and visiting the Americans was a nice weekly change of pace; Linda especially enjoyed it.

As we prepared to leave home on the fourth week, Linda suddenly didn't feel like making the trip that week. She insisted that she was okay, just tired, and I should go on by myself. I had just purchased new tires at a bargain price, for the VW minibus. It started raining lightly as I entered a winding stretch of narrow highway in a teak forest. I felt good because I had saved the mission money by buying cheaper local tires. However, the rubber the tires were made of was too hard and did not grip the road properly. So even though I was driving slower, because of the rain, the vehicle slid over into the oncoming lane.

An older truck with a load came around a curve a hundred yards away and approached. I could not get back into my lane, so decided it would be better to drive off the roadway to avoid a collision. However, though I cannot explain it, I could not turn my vehicle and get off the highway. I met the truck head-on, and the impact drove me back uphill six feet. The truck and driver were unhurt. The VW minibus was a rear-engine vehicle; thus the driver was only protected by the bumper and steering wheel.

Yet I only had minor cuts on my right hand. However, the dashboard on the passenger side was bent back into the passenger seat. Had Linda accompanied me that evening, as usual, she could have been seriously injured, and our unborn baby (Matt) possibly would not have survived.

After getting out of my vehicle, it became evident that if had I succeeded in steering the vehicle off the road to avoid the collision, I would have gone down a ten-foot incline and crashed into one of the teak trees and possibly been killed. Oh yes, just coincidence; however, although God does not cause all things, "God causes all things to work together for good to those who love Him." Our "good" is to become more like Jesus (Romans 8:28–29).

So, God prevented Linda from accompanying me, thus avoiding injury or death for her and our unborn son. He prevented me from maneuvering my vehicle off the road and near-certain death. *Many people never recognize God working around them, but that does not mean He is not there.*

After getting the vehicle repaired, I exchanged those tires with the best available tires. Since then, I always use the best tires available.

I will share one more event, an event that I did not personally witness. My children tell me this story from when we lived in Tegal. I had traveled to Semarang, by train, to attend a seminary board meeting. I left our vehicle at home with Linda. Linda got very sick with dengue fever (broken bone fever). She ran a high fever and felt miserable. Knowing that Win Applewhite, missionary doctor, was at the meeting, Linda packed our then-three kids into our vehicle and drove herself to Semarang. Along the way, she drove over a temporary bridge across a small river.

Workers were in the process of demolishing that temporary bridge because the new bridge was finished and in use. They had already removed stretches of planks. Nevertheless, Linda drove safely across that impassable temporary bridge, as workers shouted and waved their arms at her. *Did that really happen? I do not know for certain, but I believe my boys, and I never doubt God's ability.*

I could go on and on, but the several incidents of divine or angelic encounters, interventions, and interactions with us in the body of my story, as well as the five incidents in this appendix are sufficient to illustrate my claims of God interacting with mankind. I will, however, conclude this section with several more references of divine intervention in the Bible.

Ephesians 1:4–5 "He chose us in Him before the foundation of the world, that we should be holy and blameless before Him. In love He predestinated us to the adoption of sons through Jesus Christ to Himself, according to the kind intention of His will, to the praise of the glory of His grace."

"In the beginning God created the heavens and the earth" (Genesis 1:1).

"God created man in His own image, in the image of God He created him; male and female He created them. And God blessed them, and God said, 'Be fruitful and multiply, and fill the earth, and subdue it and rule over it'" (Genesis 1:27–28).

Genesis 12:1–3 "Now the LORD *said to Abram, 'Go forth from your country, and your relatives and from your father's house, to the land which I will show you; and I will make you a great nation, and I will bless you, and make your name great; and so you shall be a blessing; and I will bless those that bless you, and the one that curses you I will curse, and in you all the families of the earth shall be blessed.'"*

"In the beginning was the Word, and the Word was with God, and the Word was God" (John 1:1).

"In Him was life, and the life was the Light of men" (John 1:4).

"He was in the world, and the world was made through Him, and the world did not know Him" (John 1:10).

"But as many as received Him, to them He gave the right to become children of God, even to them that believe in His name, who were born, not of blood, nor of the will of the flesh, nor of the will of man, but of God" (John 1:12–13).

"And the Word became flesh, and dwelt among us, and we saw His glory, glory as of the only begotten from the Father, full of grace and truth" (John 1:14).

"When the fullness of time came, God sent forth His Son, born of a woman, born under the Law, so that He might redeem those who were under the Law, that we might receive the adoption as sons" (Galatians 4:4–5).

"For while we were still helpless, at the right time Christ died for the ungodly" (Romans 5:6).

"In Him we have redemption through His blood, the forgiveness of our trespasses, according to the riches of His grace" (Ephesians 1:7).

"God causes all things to work together for good to those who love God, to those who are called according to His purpose. For whom He foreknew, He also predestined to become conformed to the image of His Son" (Romans 8:28–29).

On and on, God's word reveals that He works in our behalf. We either receive His grace by faith, or we reject Him by unbelief. The ball is in our court.

Appendix B

Plans for My Funeral

I love the works of the eighteenth-century Scottish poet Robert Burns.

I am amused by his *"Ode to a Louse,"* where a proud lady sits in church with all her finery, but fellow worshipers notice a louse on her bonnet. Thus, Burns humorously laments that if we could see ourselves as others see us, we would not strut around in pride.

My favorite is an *"Ode to a Mouse,"* where a field mouse worked hard preparing and stocking his underground nest for the winter, only to have it accidently destroyed by the plough of an apologetic Burns (Burns was a farmer). The most memorable line is *"the best laid schemes of mice and men."*

My Memorial Service

My funeral/memorial service desires are a fantasy—plans that because of change and circumstance, probably can't be carried out exactly as I plan (like in the "Ode to a Mouse"), but I hereby share my fantasy.

I prefer that my body be disposed of prior to the memorial service. If casket is used, make it cheap. If cremation is used (ashes dumped in Palo Dura Canyon by family would suit me).

I would like for the service to be held in the worship center at First Baptist Church, Amarillo, Texas.

My preference is that service be led by Howie (Dr. Howard Batson).

I would like to have three soloists: Lanny Allen, Steve Bowen, and Dan Baker.

I would like Janice Davis to be pianist and David Lowe to be organist.

I would like for Dr. Clyde Meador, of Richmond, Virginia— my former IMB boss, dear friend, and mentor—to have a small part in the service.

Order of Service

Prelude to be a joyful organ and piano mini concert of praise to God, as follows (determined by Janice Davis and David Lowe):

As the family enters: "Joyful, Joyful, We Adore Thee/Ode to Joy," organ and piano duet (with gusto).

Solo: Lanny Allen, "Amazing Grace," with modern "My Chains Are Gone" ending.

Obituary and family memories: *Howie*

Dr. Clyde Meador, three to five minutes, Fred's former life as missionary.

Solo: Steve Bowen, "If It Were Not for Grace"

Homily: Howie, "It's Not about Fred, but about God and His Grace"

Solo: Dan Baker, "Lord of the Dance"

Congregation sing: "Victory in Jesus"

Organ Solo: David Lowe's special organ arrangement of "When We All Get to Heaven."

Closing Prayer by Pastor Howie

Organ and Piano: "O Zion Haste" (with gusto)

Just the thought of such a service makes my heart glad. This is what I would love, but … "the best laid plans of mice and men."

In reality, when I kneel in the presence of God, what takes place during my memorial service will be insignificant to me. Besides, funerals are for the living, not the dead.

Appendix C

In Memory of Calvin Fox

From: Fred & Linda Beck
Sent: Tuesday, December 16, 2003
To: Eric Bridges, IMB
Subject: Calvin Fox, Missionary Agriculturalist & Evangelist

Dear Eric,

We worked closely with Calvin in India for about seven years and value our friendship. We will miss him.

Calvin was a man who loved God and his fellowman. He had a passion for meeting both the physical and spiritual needs of people. He was especially drawn to the plight of subsistence farmers and their families. He understood their situation and their aspirations.

One of the keys to Calvin's success with subsistence farmers was his appreciation for their skills. Thus, he didn't try to change how they farmed. Instead, he introduced off season agriculture on wastelands and other under used land to provide additional much needed food, and/or cash crops.

Calvin's vision coupled agriculture and public health to facilitate better health and economic prosperity for the families of subsistence farmers, to open their understanding about the God who cares about them and, to thus lead them to Jesus. God especially gifted Calvin to discover, develop, or improve many simple, yet very successful agricultural techniques, which were attractive, affordable, profitable and sustainable for subsistence farmers.

Besides the obvious fact that God was at work, another key to Calvin's success was that instead of trying to do everything himself, Calvin trained and used many local agricultural technicians to extend his concepts. He also followed up with the people he trained to enable them to succeed and thereby impact the physical and spiritual needs of the masses.

Because of an especially high mortality rate among infants and small children, Calvin enlisted a local physician, with a heart for the poor, to join him in training low level village health workers to minister to simple health needs, deliver babies, teach nutrition and train mothers to plant backyard gardens to meet the nutritional needs of their family.

Those practical expressions of God's love for the people, opened their hearts to learn more about God. Calvin improved an existing program for training locals to include Chronological Bible Storying and greatly multiplied the number of Bible Story Tellers. Those Story Tellers were mainly farmers, who also served as unpaid evangelists and church planters.

As a result of all of those things, over a five-year period, we saw three church planting movements take place. Those movements produced nearly 1,000 new churches, among three separate people groups. In addition, the seeds for several more church planting movements were planted among several other unreached people groups.

Calvin will be missed by the thousands of people, whose lives were directly impacted by God through him.

About the Author

After pastoring Energy Baptist Church, Energy, Texas; Esparto Baptist Mission, Esparto, California; and First Baptist Church, Folsom, California, Fred and Linda Beck served thirty-three years, as Baptist missionaries through the International Mission Board, SBC, Richmond, Virginia.

They evangelized, planted churches, and developed local leaders for twenty years on the Indonesian islands of Java, Ambon, and Seram. Then they transferred to South Asia to help train hundreds of pastors, through itinerant seminars across rural areas and cities of India and surrounding countries, for thirteen years.

They retired in Amarillo, Texas, in 2002. Since then, both have been heavily involved in adult ESL, adult literacy among immigrants and teaching adult Bible classes at First Baptist Church, Amarillo. Fred also works in FBC's Christian Men's Job Corps and FBC's Disaster Response Ministries.

CPSIA information can be obtained
at www.ICGtesting.com
Printed in the USA
FFOW02n0329240718
47485711-50776FF